**Billy Graham**
Evangelistic Association

D0469577

Dear Friend,

I am pleased to send you this co[py] [of] [this] [book], written by my father's longtime associate Howard O. Jones.

My father asked Dr. Jones to join the Billy Graham Team in the 1950s at a time of racial tension and change that affected the entire nation. As an evangelist and powerful preacher, Dr. Jones was a pioneer on race reconciliation in the church for over half a century. I pray that this compelling story will bless your life and touch your heart.

The Billy Graham Evangelistic Association exists to take the message of Christ to all we can by every effective means available to us. Our desire is to introduce as many people as we can to the person of Jesus Christ, so that they might experience His love and forgiveness.

Your prayers are the most important way to support us in this ministry. We are grateful for the dedicated prayer support we receive. We are also grateful for those who support us with contributions.

If you would like to know more about the Billy Graham Evangelistic Association, please contact us:

In the U.S.:

Billy Graham Evangelistic Association
1 Billy Graham Parkway
Charlotte, North Carolina 28201-0001
www.billygraham.org
Toll-free: 1-877-2GRAHAM
(1-877-247-2426)

In Canada:

Billy Graham Evangelistic Association of Canada
20 Hopewell Way NE
Calgary, Alberta T3J 5H5
www.billygraham.ca
Toll-free: 1-888-393-0003

We would appreciate knowing how this book or our ministry has touched your life. May God bless you.

Sincerely,

Franklin Graham
President

Howard O. Jones, a towering figure among Christian evangelists of our time, with clarity, warmth and great passion tells his life story. Insights are given to Billy Graham's struggle to bridge the racial divide that only an insider would know. You must read this inspiring autobiography.

ELLIOT J. MASON, SR.
Co-Director, World Renewal Ministries

I have known Howard O. Jones for decades. In a unique way, God has prepared him as an evangelist-teacher to cross all racial barriers. This autobiography is a dynamic account of what God can do with a person fully surrendered to Him.

DR. GEORGE SWEETING
Chancellor Emeritus, Moody Bible Institute

The ministry of Howard O. Jones has been a blessing to me and to the hundreds of thousands of others across this country and around the world who have heard his sermons and sought to model his godly example. This book is a window into the soul of a saintly soldier for the Lord Jesus Christ. Read it and be encouraged as you travel with Dr. Jones from Oberlin, Ohio to Harlem, New York to a landmark ministry among the nations of West Africa! Here is a ministry that went "into all the world."

MARVIN A. MCMICKLE
Professor of Preaching, Ashland Theological Seminary
Pastor of Antioch Baptist Church of Cleveland, Ohio

Dr. Jones has exhorted the hearts of countless students with his passionate words: Christians need a clear view of our cities through the tear-filled eyes of a compassionate Christ. His passion has ignited the hearts of students to not be ashamed of the gospel, recognizing that it is the power of God unto salvation.

DR. GARY M. BENEDICT
President, Crown College

Gospel Trailblazer

AN AFRICAN-AMERICAN PREACHER'S HISTORIC JOURNEY ACROSS RACIAL LINES

This **Billy Graham Library Selection** is published
by the Billy Graham Evangelistic Association
with permission from Moody Publishers.

MOODY PUBLISHERS

CHICAGO

Published by the Billy Graham Evangelistic Association
with permission from Moody Publishers.

A **Billy Graham Library Selection** designates materials
that are appropriate for a well-rounded collection of
quality Christian literature, including both classic and
contemporary reading and reference materials.

ISBN 1-59328-069-6

Cover design: Smartt Guys Design
Interior design: Ragont Design

This book is dedicated to the memory of my beloved wife, Wanda; our precious children and grandchildren; and to Reverend and Mrs. Charles Mayle and the members of the Oberlin Alliance Church.

TABLE OF CONTENTS

FOREWORD

For many years, Howard Jones and I joined hands together in evangelism. We will never forget Howard's courage in joining the Billy Graham Team in the mid-1950s, at a time of great racial tension throughout the country. Since that time, we have covered many miles together, and I have scores of wonderful memories.

This book contains many of those memories—stories of the things Howard and I experienced together and of the way we saw God at work.

It has been a privilege for me to call Howard not only an associate in ministry, but also my friend. His wife, Wanda, was a great woman of God, and together they raised a wonderful family.

I commend this book to you, and I pray that it will bless your heart and impact your walk with Jesus Christ—just as Howard's ministry touched many, many people around the world as he faithfully did what God called him to do.

BILLY GRAHAM
October 3, 2002

ACKNOWLEDGMENTS

This autobiography couldn't have been written without the prayers, encouragement, and hard work of numerous people. Of course, my dear children and grandchildren walked with me every step of the way on this journey, as did Reverend Charles B. Mayle and the members of Oberlin Alliance Church.

Special thanks goes to Greg Thornton and his outstanding staff at Moody Publishers for their patience, passion, and unending belief in this book and its message.

I also must express deep gratitude to Billy and Franklin Graham, Stephanie Wills and Cathy Wood, and other members of the Billy Graham Evangelistic Association who have labored and helped me in so many ways throughout the years.

I am grateful to Edward Gilbreath for lending his gifts as a wordsmith to help me put my story on paper. And to his wife, Dana, and their two beautiful children for allowing Ed to devote so much time and sweat to this project.

A special appreciation goes to Sandra Aldrich, a dear friend who helped Wanda write her autobiography. At times, Wanda's book helped jog my memory and allowed Ed to hear my wife's voice as it sounded before she became ill.

Thanks to my dear friends and preaching colleagues Warren Wiersbe, Stephen Olford, Elliot J. Mason, James Earl

Massey, Ralph Bell, Ron Ballard, Ernest Brown, Alphonso Tyler, Bob Harrison, Walter Arties, and others for their counsel and prayers. And to another friend, the late Reverend A.T. Rowan, the former pastor of Bethany Baptist Church in Cleveland, Ohio.

Dr. and Mrs. Bradley Brown, Southern Baptist Missionaries to Liberia, West Africa.

Maurice Shave and the staff at Savannah Corporation in Northridge, Ohio; Dr. Glen Plumer, CEO and President of National Religious Broadcasters; and friend George Parsons, who has given me such great advice over the years.

To Moody Radio, for airing my program, the *Hour of Freedom,* for years over many of your stations.

To Dr. Morgan J. Hodges, and Reverend Warren Shelton who helped me with the *Soldiers for Christ Radio Ministry* in New York City, in 1944.

To Ted Smith, BGEA pianist, who helped my daughters, The Jones Sisters Trio, record their first record album.

To Jimmy McDonald who was the first soloist to join me in meetings in New York City and Philadelphia years ago.

To Huntley Brown who dedicated the song "Lift Every Voice" to my wife and me on his newest CD, "God Bless America."

To the directors of the Billy Graham Schools of Evangelism over the years for allowing me to preach the Word of God in morning sessions and lead an afternoon seminar on "How to Give an Invitation."

To Welcome Nursing Home in Oberlin, Ohio for taking care of my wife, Wanda, and other members of my family.

To my son, David, who shares one of his songs on the CD of this book.

David Poyer, Professor of Economics at Morehouse College in Atlanta, GA.

Oh, and there are so many other loved ones in my extended family I could mention if only time and space had permitted.

Dr. and Mrs. Archibald Grierson, longtime friends and supporters of our ministry.

An appreciation to the African American Alliance Women Missionaries, Donna Batise and Nysa Costa, who served so well for the Lord in West Africa, may God give us more black Alliance missionaries in the near future.

Finally, a word of thanks to the National Association of Negro Business and Professional Women's Club, Inc. of Oberlin, Ohio for presenting the National Sojourner Truth Award to Wanda Jones on March 10, 1990 for her meritorious community service, and deep concern advancing the status of women.

On March 9, 2002, I received the Frederick Douglass Award from the same organization.

Finally to Russ Busby, the chief photographer for the Billy Graham team, who took many pictures for the book.

INTRODUCTION

The Heart *of an* Evangelist
To Heal a Divided World

O n a humid morning in late June 2002, I hopped in a car with a friend and embarked on the 230-mile trip southward from Oberlin, Ohio, to Cincinnati. I don't travel as much as I used to, and even if I did, Cincinnati is not a city I have much cause to visit these days. But on this day I wanted to go there. My friend and former employer Billy Graham was in town, and we needed to talk.

What brought Billy to the area was the Greater Cincinnati/Northern Kentucky evangelistic crusade (or "mission," as they're now called). More than 200,000 people were predicted to attend the event, which many expected would be one of Billy's final appearances, given his increasingly fragile health. What set this crusade apart from most others was the backdrop of racial unrest that plagued the city of Cincinnati.

A year earlier, in April 2001, a nineteen-year-old black man named Timothy Thomas refused to halt when approached by a Cincinnati police officer and was shot and killed as a result. Thomas, it turned out, had been unarmed. Had it been just an isolated occurrence, the incident might have gone unnoticed. After all, the Over-the-Rhine neighborhood where the shooting took place was a predominantly African-American community where frequent interactions between law enforcement and alleged lawbreakers was not uncommon. But Thomas's death marked the fifteenth police killing of a black man since 1995, and the fourth since November 2000. The African-American community was incensed—and tired.

Three days after the killing, the city was put on edge as an already tragic situation took a bad turn. What began as angry protests by black citizens erupted into a full-blown race riot. A crowd, which at one point swelled to nearly eight hundred people, threw rocks and bottles at police officers. They looted stores, broke windows, and set fire to a market in the heart of the city. Police fired tear gas and rubber bullets at the demonstrators. A citywide curfew was initiated, and the people of Cincinnati became prisoners in their own homes.

The angry crowds dwindled after a few hours, but not before dozens of people were injured, and at least twenty were arrested on charges of disorderly conduct. It was the end of the rioting, but the beginning of a long soul-searching that catapulted Cincinnati into the national spotlight as the latest symbol of racial division in America.

In the months that followed, the city attempted to heal itself in a number of ways—some of them more constructive than others. Community groups formed to discuss the issues of racial profiling, police brutality, and social injustice that had contributed to the uprising. Churches worked harder to reach across racial lines as an example to the city. But several community activists who, dissatisfied with the city's response to the implicit racism displayed by the Cincinnati police, called for a boycott of the city's hotels, entertainment venues, and other revenue-generating institutions. Many in Cincinnati's black community supported the boycott, and many national entertainers—of all races—canceled engagements in Cincinnati as a show of support.

Billy's Cincinnati crusade had been on the docket long before the racial turmoil in the city. When Billy was asked by activists to observe the boycott and cancel his Cincinnati rally, he gave it serious thought. But after much prayer, he and his team decided that, more than ever, it was important for the event to go on as planned. And, ignoring the pressure of boycotters, most African-American church leaders in the community agreed with his decision.

"We're trying to bring healing to the city of Cincinnati," said the Reverend Damon Lynch Jr., a local pastor who was a cochair of the crusade. "What we're dealing with is mission and evangelism—not politics."

And so Billy went to Cincinnati, despite the pressure to stay away. There had been many other times when Billy followed his heart and did what he believed to be right, regardless of public or political pressure. One of those times was when he brought me on board his evangelistic team forty-five years earlier.

THE JACKIE ROBINSON MODEL

In 1957 I was a young black pastor with a heart for evangelism, and Billy had reached a point in his ministry where he was convinced that God wanted him to integrate his organization. No amount of words on this page could underscore enough how risky and noteworthy it was for a prominent white preacher such as Billy Graham to mess with the racial conventions of the day. Yet Billy did. And consequently, I became the first black evangelist on his team—and really the first African American to fill a high-profile role within a white evangelical organization.

When Christianity Today magazine did a story on me a few years ago, they called me "the Jackie Robinson of American evangelism." I didn't like that title then. I had never thought about what I've done in my life and ministry in terms of race. I'm a black man. That's an indisputable fact. But the gospel of Jesus Christ has always transcended whatever racial or cultural boundaries we've constructed to limit it. I've preached to white crowds, black crowds, African crowds, British crowds, Asian crowds, Hispanic crowds, Native American crowds, and the list goes on. I'll preach anywhere God takes me and to anyone He places before me.

Still, after pondering it, I grew to appreciate the Jackie Robinson comparison. Robinson was more than a baseball player. As the first black ballplayer to integrate the Major Leagues in 1947, he became a symbol for the hope of racial progress in America.

When Brooklyn Dodgers owner Branch Rickey decided to add a black player to his team's roster, he knew it would be a controversial move. The famous account of Rickey's initial meeting with Robinson plays out like an early scene from an epic war movie—except this was real life, and the battlefield would be a ball diamond. Rickey warned Robinson that it wouldn't be easy, that he would be called hurtful names and be on the receiving end of physical taunts and wild pitches aimed at his head. Rickey tested Robinson by playing the role of a foul-mouthed bigot. He got in the ballplayer's face and spewed a sampling of some of the epithets he'd likely hear. Then he reportedly took a swing at Robinson, but missed.

Rickey had made his point, though. "You're going to have to put up with a lot of this kind of stuff," he told Robinson.

The tall, athletic black man was clearly wound up by Rickey's no-holds-barred role-playing. "Well, Mr. Rickey, do you want a player who doesn't have the guts to fight back?" he said. And that's when Rickey delivered his most memorable line: "Jackie, I want a ballplayer with the guts not to fight back."

And thus began baseball's historic "experiment" in integration. As Rickey had predicted, the epithets did come, as did the bean balls, and physical taunts. Through it all, Robinson's task was to turn the other cheek. And because he did, he opened the door for other black athletes to integrate professional sports in America. But more importantly, his example provided a model of hope that transcended baseball and sports and inspired a generation to have the guts to confront the ugly institution of racism in every part of our society.

I don't pretend to have the courage of a Jackie Robinson. After all, I was not in a position every night where I faced the prospect of errant fastballs zooming toward my head. But I do thank God that He used me to open new doors for the preaching of His Word in places both near (white American churches) and far (the bush countries of West Africa). I have no doubt God placed me where He did. It was not by my doing.

The truth is, God hates the way we've commandeered

race and culture to divide ourselves and set one group up as better than others. And when one of His influential servants does something radical to buck the status quo—the way Billy Graham did when he named me as one of his associates—I believe it should be remembered.

That's one of the reasons I felt strongly about getting to Cincinnati to see Billy that hot June in 2002. Once again, he found himself at the center of a controversy simply because he was being faithful to the call of the gospel. I wanted to encourage him to remember the great odds we were able to overcome so many years earlier and encourage him to continue to do what he knows is right. I also knew it might be one of the last opportunities for Billy and me to see each other.

A FLOOD OF MEMORIES

So I decided to make the trip south to attend one evening's crusade. My friend Maurice Shave, a successful North Ridgeville, Ohio businessman with an enormous heart for God, was my driving buddy. Actually, he was the driver. At eighty-two, I can still do the driving I need to do around my hometown of Oberlin. But for longer road trips, or when it involves negotiating the twists and turns at the airport to pick up a friend or family member, Maurice is always there to help.

When we arrived in Cincinnati, a few boycotters stood outside Paul Brown Stadium, protesting the event. But their presence did not discourage the tens of thousands of people who flocked into the venue to worship, pray, and hear God's Word.

I was able to visit briefly with Billy before the program. We laughed together and reminisced about all the great history we shared. He told me his earthly frame was getting weaker. "Howard, I'm looking forward to heaven," he said. He knew I could relate. I encouraged him to stay focused on the Good News, despite all the obvious distractions.

As Maurice and I drove home the next morning, a flood of memories filled my mind: good times with Billy; a lifetime of joy and fulfillment with my dear wife, Wanda, who had passed away in November; the faces of countless men and women, boys and girls who came forward to receive Christ as a result of my preaching, even on those many occasions when I felt like I had fumbled the message. There were travels to Africa, Korea, England, France, South America, Switzerland, Brazil—you name it.

I cannot begin to recall every locale I've visited and every person I've met during my fifty-plus years of ministry. Yet in the pages that follow I endeavor to give you at least a glimpse—a quick taste—of the incredible adventure and excitement that have accompanied my journeys as a pastor, missionary, and evangelist.

It's been said that old preachers never die; they just ramble on and on and on.

Are you ready to ramble?

PART ONE
Beginnings

ONE

The Start *of* Me

MEMORIES OF FAMILY, FUN AND FAITH

I could not believe my ears. Wanda Young, the one girl in all the world with whom I wanted to spend the rest of my life, had dumped me.

It was 1940, and I was a rising young musician in a popular dance band with a bright future. I had just asked Wanda to be my wife. I promised her fame and fortune, because I was sure one day my band would be known from coast to coast as one of the great swing orchestras. I had earned a reputation around Cleveland as a blazing young talent on the clarinet and alto saxophone. But Wanda was not impressed. Nor was she swept off her feet by my dreams of our future together. She had other ideas—ideas that were radically different from mine.

"Howard," she said, "even though I love you, I love Christ more. Therefore, unless you accept Jesus Christ as your personal Savior, I will not be able to see you anymore, because we'll have nothing more in common with each other."

What? How strange these words sounded coming out of my girlfriend's seventeen-year-old mouth. She spoke in that same tender and sweet voice I had grown to adore. But this time there was an unmistakable edge to her tone. It was an edge that left no doubt in my mind: This young woman was not kidding. Her seriousness was neither impersonal nor arrogant. It was just a matter of fact. She was telling the truth. God had done something profound in her heart. Sadly, I was still too caught up in my own hopes and ambitions to understand that.

What did she mean about accepting Jesus Christ as my personal Savior? Hadn't I been there and done that? *After all,* I thought, *I was just as religious as she was. Wasn't I a member of a church? Hadn't I been baptized? Wasn't that enough religion for one man?*

Not enough for Wanda. She had taken her "religion" to a new level. As I argued with myself for a response to her words, she challenged me further by saying, "Now that I am saved, I have a strong conviction that God has something better for you in life than a career in the dance orchestra business."

Despite her gentle appearance, she spoke with the firmness of a woman who had made up her mind. "God has shown me this jazz orchestra and all that goes with it does not really glorify Him," she said. "So, I am going to pray for your conversion, that God would deliver you from the dance band."

Whoa, now let's hold on a minute! Deliver me from the dance band? Deliver me from my dream? I wasn't sure I liked that prayer. But what could I say?

Listening to Wanda's words that night, I felt the answer to

her prayers would be the end of me. Instead, it proved to be the real beginning of Howard Jones.

THE ROOTS OF THE MATTER

Before I go any farther, I suppose I should back up and tell you a little bit about where I come from. Then, perhaps, you'll understand better the slow and steady dance God used to woo me to Himself. The fact that He used the influence of a beautiful young woman to get through to me, in retrospect, was a nice touch. However, back then it felt like I was being squeezed in a vice grip.

I was born April 12, 1921, in Cleveland, Ohio. It was there I spent my boyhood and started school. My musical career began in Cleveland, as well. My father, Howard O. Jones Sr., was a lover of music and encouraged my younger brother, Clarence, and me to learn to play musical instruments by the time we were eight and six. I chose the clarinet; Clarence chose the trumpet.

My father was a plasterer by trade. I'll always remember his big, brown, calloused hands and how firm yet gentle they could be. My mother, Josephine Jones, was a wonderful woman. Besides taking care of Clarence and me, she worked as a housekeeper. After we got a little older, she opened her own beauty parlor.

We lived on the east side of Cleveland. My dad's mother, Mary Mungeon, lived in Oberlin, the picturesque little town thirty-five miles southwest of Cleveland that is home to the famous abolitionist school Oberlin College, which for a time, during the 1800s, claimed the legendary revivalist Charles Finney as president.

My ancestors had arrived in Cleveland fifteen years after the Civil War. My great-grandmother Jane Martin had been born into slavery on a Virginia plantation, but she dreamed of going north one day and dipping her hands in the waters of Lake Erie. For her, that would be a way of knowing she was finally free.

After the war, the Emancipation Proclamation granted freedom to the slaves. In time, my great-grandmother, a woman of courage and action, mobilized her husband, Henry, their two daughters (the youngest of whom was my grandmother, Mary), and other extended family members and made the trek northward. "Someday you'll drink from Lake Erie," she promised her daughters.

So by foot, oxcart, train, and boat, the family finally arrived in Ohio in April 1881. They had no friends, no place to stay, and little money, but they had each other and were getting ever closer to fulfilling my great-grandmother's vision. Grandma Mary remembers her mom's reassurances: "Jesus is with us and will provide for us," Jane Martin would say. Then she'd begin to sing, "Where He leads me, I will follow."

After short stopovers in Huntington and Cincinnati, the Martin family did make it to Cleveland, where they triumphantly walked the shores of Lake Erie. And, oh yes, they took a drink!

Two years later, the family moved to Oberlin, where they joined other black families in organizing the historic Mount Zion Baptist Church. There were about four hundred black folk in Oberlin at that time—one-fifth of the population—and my ancestors soon took a prominent role among the Negroes of the community.

My great-grandparents died in the early 1900s. Grandma

Mary, who was twenty years old when her family moved to Oberlin, had married my grandfather, Goglin Jones, in Cleveland before settling in Oberlin. A wig maker (and all-around businesswoman), Grandmother Mary ran a shop on Main Street in Oberlin. After my grandfather's death, she went on to marry Samuel Mungeon. Samuel Mungeon was an interesting fellow—6'3", 250 pounds. He was a farmer through and through. He ate a bowl of rice every morning and credited that habit for his sturdy health. He was from the Deep South and couldn't read or write. But he had a good heart and taught us practical life lessons.

Grandma Mungeon built two beautiful homes on Quebec Avenue in Cleveland—one in the front and a two-family structure that sat farther back on the lot. We lived in the first house, and the second house was rented out. Grandma asked her son, my dad, to manage the property, which he did.

CHILDHOOD REFLECTIONS

Our neighborhood was a lovely, middle-class community. It was an integrated neighborhood. That's not to say there wasn't racial friction in our community—but more on that later.

Clarence and I grew up knowing children of different races. Across the street and to the left of us, lived Italian families. To the right of us, lived a black family. On the corner, there was a Jewish store. In another section of the neighborhood, there were Bohemian families. We grew up playing with kids of different cultures and colors. As I look back, I'm thankful for that because it prepared me for the many cross-cultural situations I've faced throughout my ministry.

Clarence and I were generally good kids. We'd get into

mischief like any other little boys, but our parents instilled in us a good sense of right and wrong. Our rebellion was the short-lived kind that was easily cured by a swift spanking.

Our "running buddies" were the boys from next door and across the street. We had a great time playing ball, shooting marbles—you name it. Occasionally, we'd get into a scrap if someone attempted to cheat in a game or for some other forgettable cause. But for the most part, we were a united group—black, Italian, German, Bohemian. If a strange kid wandered into the neighborhood and attempted to "put us in our place" by calling the black kids "niggers," we'd all beat him up and send him flying out of our area. Our social contract didn't allow much room for racial ugliness.

We enjoyed visiting our grandparents in Oberlin. Oberlin was a smaller town, yet there seemed to be more to do there for two young boys who loved to run in the woods and play baseball.

One summer we were visiting our grandparents in Oberlin, when Grandpa Mungeon recruited us to help him with farm work. On this particular August day, we had plans to participate in a ball game down at the park grounds. But Grandpa Mungeon had other plans. "I want you boys to come out and we're going to plant some late corn," he said. Late corn was the variety of the plant that was sowed for a late-summer harvest.

"But, Grandpa, we got a game at around one o'clock," I said. But the urgency of our appointment failed to impress Grandpa Mungeon.

"Your ball game can wait," he said. "You're going to plant corn."

And that was the end of it.

So we went out to the cornfield, and he gave us buckets of corn seeds that had been soaking in water overnight. This made them very soft.

This was the plan: Grandpa would form several rows with his hoe, making holes at regular intervals. Our job was to drop three kernels of corn in each hole and cover them up with soil using our spades.

Grandpa took his hoe and formed three long rows of holes for us to plant the seeds in, and then he went on the other end of the field. Resigned to our fate, Clarence and I went to work, putting three kernels of corn in each hole and covering them. We had nearly completed the second lane when the sun really started to beat down on us. Grandpa was prepared, though. He signaled us to take a break and brought us cups of cold lemonade. This provided temporary relief—but it was still brutally hot and getting hotter. So I devised a plan. I said to my brother, "Clarence, let's start putting four kernels of corn in each hole." He liked that idea, too.

Our grandfather, in the meantime, was admiring our handiwork from afar. "How are you boys doing?" he hollered from across the field.

"Oh, fine," we replied, trying to conceal our satisfaction over the new planting system we'd engineered.

"When you finish that pail of corn, then we'll knock off, get some lunch, and then you boys can go play ball," Grandpa said.

We smiled and started dropping even more seeds in the holes—four became five, five became six, until soon we were dumping fistfuls of corn in the remaining holes. In no time our bucket was empty, and we were released to eat lunch and play ball.

We went home to Cleveland the next day. And of course, we never told Grandpa about our little timesaving technique. We didn't have to.

A couple of weeks later, Grandpa was tending to his fields when he noticed something peculiar about his corn crop. "I see some of my corn is coming up great," he said to himself. "But what happened up here?" As he moved through the field, the corn went from perfect single stalks to weedlike bushes of the plant. His crop was ruined. It didn't take him long at all to know what had happened. "Those little rascals," he said.

Needless to say, Grandpa was angry. The sun was beating down, just as it had been two weeks earlier. And he just stood there, massaging his forehead with one hand, leaning on his hoe with the other. Later, he told us his first thought was, "Oh, I'd like to get those rascals. I'd wear their bottoms out." But then he started laughing. And he called my dad and told him what happened. He said, "Howard, don't whip them. I guess I worked them too hard."

If only Dad had taken his advice.

There were darker memories, too. A few blocks away from our home in Cleveland was a large bakery that specialized in cookies and breads. On a nice day, you could smell the sweet aroma of freshly baked oatmeal cookies drifting in the air.

On one side of the bakery there was a store where people from the neighborhood bought day-old goods. On the other side of the building was a dumping area where the bakery would leave its garbage and refuse materials for the city to pick up. One summer day, when I was about ten, my brother and I and a couple of our friends were exploring this dumping ground, poking through the trash with sticks, looking for some "buried treasure." We were having a good time. Then I saw it—a large shoebox that looked like it had just come off a department store shelf. And when I mindlessly kicked the box, it felt like there might still be a pair of shoes inside.

Thinking I had hit the mother lode, I picked up the box and removed the lid to see what looked like a white baby doll. It was adorned in a pretty little dress with a cute hat on its head and pink booties on its feet. I wondered why such a nice doll would be left in this dump. But when I touched the doll's cheek, I knew that it was not a doll but a real little person—a lifeless baby girl. I stepped back in fear, and without thinking dropped the shoebox. I called Clarence and the other boys over to show them my discovery. We were all frightened.

I ran to get my father. When he arrived, he examined the shoebox's contents. He could tell immediately that it was a baby. "Some poor woman has discarded her child," he said.

Dad called the police. They briefly questioned us, and then took the little body away. We imagined that we would eventually read about the police's investigation in the paper, but we never heard anything about it again.

To this day, I can see the image of that precious little girl, dressed so beautifully, abandoned in a shoebox coffin. Nowadays, you hear about discarded babies being discovered all the time. When I hear these reports, it breaks my heart in the deepest way. But back then, for a wide-eyed little boy, it was especially jarring. I remember saying to myself how glad I was that my mother and father hadn't thrown my brother and me away when we were born.

I can't think of any kids I grew up with who did not have fathers at home. There might have been one or two exceptions, but as a rule all the dads in our community took care of their children. Our neighborhood was composed of loving families—not perfect ones, of course. But, unlike so many neighborhoods today, we had community. Everybody looked out for everyone else. The lawns were maintained, flowers were planted around each home, and everyone took pride in his house. That meant a lot to us.

Mind you, this was during the Great Depression. Money was scarce, jobs were in short supply, and the value of a daily meal was not taken for granted. Some of the people worked hard to make do on what little they could afford.

Still, in our neighborhood we didn't have any slums. The people sacrificed. The fathers went out and got jobs. Sometimes the mothers had to work. Whatever was required, those men and women found the fortitude to do it. They gave all they had for their families.

Once in a while you'd see somebody come through the neighborhood begging for food or money. We used to see quite a few beggars come down our street. And there's one thing I remember about my mother. She would never turn anyone away. I remember one day when a man came to our front door and said, "I'm hungry." Mother said, "All right, just sit there on the steps and I'll bring you something." She brought him a sandwich and a cup of water. And other families in the neighborhood did that, as well.

Our parents taught us to never turn away anyone who is in need, because you may be in need someday yourself. Mother would tell us, "God has blessed us, so we need to share those blessings with others." We didn't have a lot, but I never knew a time when Clarence and I wanted for anything. Of course, my Grandma and Grandpa Mungeon were nearby in Oberlin, and their little farm was a source of a lot of good meals. From time to time, they would come up to Cleveland and bring us vegetables and other crops.

Those were tough times, but they were sweet.

Today, that east side neighborhood is still there. It's not the greatest neighborhood in Cleveland, nor is it the worst. And the house we grew up in is still standing. I often hope the families that have lived there since we did have been as happy as we were.

LIFE WITH DAD

Dad worked. If he couldn't find a job plastering, he found something else. He loved to whistle. I recall the many times he'd wake up early in the morning, give Clarence and me big hugs, and then give Mother a big hug. He'd say, "Well, I'm going out to scout this morning." That meant he was going out to find a job. You could hear his sharp, melodious whistle as he got in his car and drove away. Sure enough, he'd find employment every time.

Dad often told Clarence and me, "I can't stand men who won't take care of their children. Any father that doesn't take care of his children, I have no patience for." And that stuck with us.

Even though he was a busy man, our father always found time to spend with his sons. Sometimes Clarence and I would be out shooting marbles or spinning tops, and Dad would come out and get on the ground with us. Or maybe we'd be flying kites in the spring when the wind was good, and he'd come out there. Our home became the "headquarters" for the neighborhood. Dad made sure we had plenty of baseball bats, gloves, and other items to share with the other kids.

One of our favorite activities with Dad was going to the ballpark. We'd go to Lunar Park in Cleveland to watch the Negro League teams. We'd see ballplayers such as Satchel Paige and Josh Gibson, incredible athletes who were not allowed to play in Major League baseball because of their skin color. Dad would take us to see them and teach us to be proud of our heritage, not to think less of ourselves because of our race.

An army man, Dad was a veteran of World War I. He did his time overseas, although he admitted he didn't like it too much. His nickname in the service had been "Cookie," because he was a cook. That tag stayed with him.

Dad didn't go far in school, but he could read and write. He told Clarence and me, as we were growing up, that education had to be one of our top priorities. He said, "You are Negro,"—that's what they called us back then—"and the only way you're going to make it in this country is to get your education. You've got to go to school and study what the white boys and girls are studying and also study your own African history and be proud of who God made you to be."

Then he would take his index finger, tap his temple, and say, "You've got to get it up here. You can't fool around and not do well in school. We've come this far through blood, sweat, and tears."

School, school, school. He drilled it into us.

Though our childhood was mostly idyllic, it wasn't impervious to the pangs of racism. One winter day, when I was about nine, some boys and I were sledding down a slope that ended outside a corner meat market in our neighborhood.

We were having a great time until I came down the hill particularly fast and wiped out in front of the store. And I remember this clerk rushed out, a white man. He said, "You niggers. Get away from my store." And he picked up a hard, frozen clump of snow and flung it at us, hitting me in my back. Boy, it really hurt. I cried, and I picked up my sled and ran home.

As I ran into the yard, my dad said, "What's wrong, Howard?"

"I was sliding over there by that store and that white man came out and threw a big piece of ice and hit me," I explained frantically.

My father grabbed my hand and said, "Come on."

We walked swiftly back to the store and went inside. "Good afternoon," Dad said to the man. "Did you hit my son with a clump of snow?"

"Yeah. I told those kids to stay away from in front of my store," the man said angrily.

So Dad said, "All right, that's reasonable. But all you needed to do was tell me, and I would have seen to it that they wouldn't have been playing around in front of your shop. But you should not have hit my son."

"Well, I'll hit him again if I catch him in front of my store," the man smirked, as if to say, *What are you going to do about it?*

The next thing I know, my dad had leveled the guy with a left uppercut. The man was knocked flat on his behind. He didn't know what had hit him. Then my dad helped him back to his feet. He was visibly shaking.

"Like I was saying, don't you ever hit my son again," Dad reiterated. "Please tell me when my kids are doing something wrong, but don't touch them."

"No, no. I'm sorry," the man quickly said. "I'll never do that again."

And then we left.

When we got back home, Dad told Clarence and me, "Don't you go by that store anymore." And even though we missed out on one of the best sledding slopes in the neighborhood, we listened to our father.

Clarence and I knew Dad was fearless. He never picked a fight, but he could not stomach ugliness—whether it was from a prejudiced white man or anyone else. And you were *really* asking for it if you harmed his family. He was a proud man—proud of his marriage and proud of his sons. Dad wasn't a Christian then, but he was religious—religious and indefatigably honest and good.

THE WHISTLER'S MOTHER

Like Dad, my mother was a whistler. In fact, I think she was the better one in the family. She loved to whistle, and that's where I picked up the habit. If you talk to my kids today, they'll say, "Yeah, Dad went around the house whistling all the time." It has become second nature to me because of my mom.

Josephine Jones was a remarkable woman. She was fair in complexion (due, in part, to the Cherokee and Irish blood in her family lineage), so much so that at times various whites would not believe she was a Negro. Mom, in fact, was accepted into the Cleveland School of Cosmetology, which didn't admit blacks, because she was able to "pass" as a white woman. (By the way, Mom went on to become one of the best students in the school. She graduated with her license and partnered with a friend to open a beauty parlor on the corner of 100th Street and Cedar in Oberlin.)

She loved her kids lavishly, but she never spoiled us. We never talked back, and we always knew who was in charge. "You're to take orders from us," she'd say. "You don't run this house." She taught us to respect our elders and to not interrupt when adults were speaking. And then there was this one: "Someday when you grow up and have children, you'll understand some of the things we're saying." And of course, she was right.

Mom provided the religious foundation for our family. She was a strong Christian woman. I remember when she was a member of St. James A.M.E. Church in Cleveland. It was a huge church on the east side of town. My dad had been raised as a Baptist, so he usually did not go with her. Some Sundays Clarence and I would go to St. James with Mom, some Sundays we'd stay home with Dad.

One Sunday, however, Dad took us to see Mom when she got baptized. I was seven or eight at the time. The sanctuary was packed, and I remember they had this beautiful baptismal fountain up front. The women were on one side and the men on the other, and one by one they'd take their turns getting baptized. They all wore brilliant white robes. When they brought my mother down into the fount, I remember seeing the preacher waving and delivering his little liturgy. Everything was OK until he dunked my mother under the water. I jumped up and hollered, "Don't you hurt my mother!"

The churchgoers were at first shocked, then they burst out in laughter. Dad had told me that we were going to Mom's baptism service, but he had not gone into all the details.

A few years later, thanks to Mom's influence, we started

going to church as a family every Sunday. Perhaps to make it easier on my dad, Mom switched her affiliation to East Mount Zion Baptist, which became "our church."

As I grew, I began to like church more and more. But not necessarily for the right reasons.

TWO

All That Jazz

MY BIG FAT MUSICAL DREAMS

Mom and Dad taught us that every Sunday was the Lord's Day, and that Saturday night was the time to get ready for the Lord's Day—to get our Sunday clothes arranged, take a bath, and study our lessons for Sunday school. Still, my religious life as a boy in Cleveland was a rather nominal one. My real interest in the church wasn't so much worshiping God and studying His Word, but playing in the church orchestra.

Around this time, both Clarence and I were getting pretty good on our instruments. We were taking weekly lessons and learning our way around a lot of great classical music scores.

I enjoyed the clarinet, though my first choice had been the alto saxophone. I loved the cool, mellow sound of that instrument. My idol was Johnny Hodges, a sax player who had songs like "Jeep Blues" and "On the Sunny Side of the

Street" that were out of sight. However, my dad's brother, Albert Jones, who had been a first clarinetist in the Negro Symphony Orchestra of Chicago, urged my dad to make me take up the clarinet. "They don't use saxophones in symphony orchestras," Uncle Albert said. "You start that boy on the clarinet, and if he ever wants to play a saxophone, he'll have the foundation to do it." And so, despite my initial protest, I became a clarinetist.

Clarence and I got better, and we began getting invitations to play at other churches. We played duets and were identified as promising young musicians.

A few years later, when Clarence and I entered our teens, our parents decided to move the family to Oberlin, which was fine by us. My brother and I continued to study music and took special training from professors at the Oberlin Conservatory.

I played clarinet in the Oberlin High School band. And later Clarence and I accepted an invitation to join a local dance band. Grandma Mungeon bought me a new alto saxophone, and I became the first saxophonist in this newly formed nine-member jazz orchestra headed by Wesley Stewart, a fine musician who worked at Oberlin College.

Soon we were playing for dances, parties, school proms, and nightclubs. I was thrilled, because I had dreamed of someday becoming a famous jazz musician.

Sharply decked out in white shirts, gray jackets, and black trousers, our band traveled throughout Ohio and into Pennsylvania. We played for both white and black audiences, and it gave us a sense of fulfillment and power to see people enjoying our music. Some crowds would dance, while others would sit there bobbing their heads. But the common factor was that we were in control—our music provided pleasure, entertainment, and escape for a variety of different folks.

ON THE WILD SIDE

Of course, when we played outside of churches, we were not always guaranteed a trouble-free performing environment. In fact, a lot of the clubs and parties where we entertained could get downright dangerous.

There was one dance that started off fine enough. We were playing a smooth song, couples were swaying, and everything seemed to be all right. Then suddenly, a heavyset woman burst into the dance hall and caused a commotion. Apparently, she saw her husband in the arms of another woman. And, man, was she furious! In one swift motion, she picked up a large clock off of a counter and hurled it at her husband. I guess you could say time was flying. The clock hit him in his back, and when he turned around, she began to chase him around the room. The scene escalated into a free-for-all, with people screaming, cheering her on, and throwing glasses, ashtrays, and whatever other objects they could put their hands on. If you haven't already figured it out, most of the people at that dance were pretty sufficiently tanked up with booze.

Meanwhile, our band continued to swing away, until it became obvious that this thing was getting out of hand. So we grabbed our instruments and took cover under some tables until the chaos subsided.

It was a wild night, but we still loved the lifestyle. Most of the time, our gigs were not as dramatic.

The music of the jazz world had me in its grip. I was a slave to it. Even now, I recall the many times I would stand on a dance floor listening to an outstanding orchestra play and wishing it were mine. I actually prayed to God that one day He would enable me to lead a famous orchestra, like Duke Ellington, Count Basie, and others.

My brother got a chance to play with Basie. Clarence was a great trumpeter, and a few years after leaving our group he joined the U.S. Army and played in the military band down in Fort McClellan, Alabama, where he was stationed. He got to play with some of Count Basie's band members down there, and he was so good that they passed the word on to Basie. One day, after he left the service, he got a call from Basie himself asking him to join his band in New York. My brother, however, had started a family by then and didn't have a great interest in leaving home.

Still, back in the day, circa 1939, we were both obsessed with becoming renowned players. I knew in my heart that I would one day be playing before enthusiastic crowds at places such as the Apollo Theatre in Harlem. I wanted it all— the fame, the money, the excitement of traveling the world with my horn. No one had bigger musical dreams than I had.

GOD WALTZES IN

About this time, a series of evangelistic meetings were held at my grandparents' church, Mount Zion Baptist in Oberlin where my mom and dad had also become members. One evening my brother and I and several friends attended the service. That night the evangelist preached a powerful sermon. He warned the congregation about sin and the need of getting right with God. Moved emotionally, I, along with my brother and some other friends, went forward after the service. The Christians gathered around and prayed for us.

As I knelt at the altar that night, I felt I should join the church and be baptized. I was sure if I did that, it would ensure me a place in heaven when I died. When we rose to our feet, the pastor and people began to shake our hands and rejoice that we had agreed to be baptized and become members of the church.

But one woman went deeper than mere congratulations. She called me aside and said, "Howard, I am so glad you are going to be baptized and become a member of the church. You will be giving up the dance orchestra now, won't you?"

Her question caught me off guard; but I answered her right away, because I had no intention of doing any such thing. "No, I am not going to leave the dance orchestra," I answered. "There is nothing wrong with it. I have studied music very hard. Now this opportunity has come to me, and I'm going to stick with it. I want to become a famous band leader someday."

Actually, I still did not know what it meant to be saved from sin, to be born again and live a separate life for the Lord Jesus Christ. I was only performing an outward ceremony without any inward conviction.

One month later we attended a Sunday night baptismal service. The church was filled to capacity. As the service began, the people who wanted to be baptized moved slowly one by one to the pool. I waited eagerly for my turn.

At last my brother and I were immersed. After coming out of the water, we hurried back to the dressing room and changed our clothes. With our heads still wet, we went out the back door of the church and into a waiting car and sped away to play for a big dance. But as we drove along, to my

surprise, a strange feeling of guilt overwhelmed me. I realized in my heart that what we were doing was wrong. With
effort, I pushed the feeling aside and soon lost myself in our
discussion of the big dance gig.

Time passed by swiftly for me in those days. The orchestra
was already becoming popular, and we filled more and more
important engagements. We were now in the public eye, and
we gloried in the good feeling it gave us. We reveled in the
great reviews we got in the local press. At last, it was as
though we were on our way up the ladder to musical success. The future was bright.

Then, suddenly, everything started to go wrong. Or should
I say go right?

THREE

Wanda

THE WOMAN WHO CHANGED MY DIRECTION

I'm convinced that when God brings a man and a woman together, it's not just so they can love each other and populate the world with beautiful offspring—though that is a wonderful part of the package. When God brings a man and a woman together, ultimately His purpose is to unite two people who can serve and glorify Him more as a team than as separate individuals. Of course, sometimes God can do more with a person when he's single. But often, He prefers to join two of His children together as one to accomplish His plans. I'm glad He operates that way, because I needed Wanda Young.

Wanda was a beautiful girl. There's no other way to say it. She had flawless brown skin, a dynamite smile, pretty eyes, and a perfect figure. But more than that, she carried herself like a true lady. Everyone who knew her loved her.

I had dated several girls during my high school years. As a jazz musician, I tended to attract a lot of attention. But Wanda attracted mine. When I saw her, I recognized more than a pretty face. There was something special about her demeanor that infected my heart, and the only remedy was to get to know this sweet girl better.

She was one of nine children—six boys and three girls—from a fine Oberlin family. Her father, James Young, was the lead cook at the cafeteria of the Oberlin Theological Seminary. He looked like a cook—large stomach, kind face. Her mother, Florie, was a godly woman who died when Wanda was just twelve. This left Wanda's father in a terrible depression from which he would never fully recover. But Wanda's older brother, Alden, stepped in admirably to help raise Wanda and her older sister Ruth. Two of Wanda's remaining siblings had died at young ages, the other four had moved on to college and work and the military.

Oberlin was a small community, so Wanda knew who I was. In fact, her parents had been good friends with my grandparents years before. She knew I played in the high school band. But early on she didn't appear to have eyes for me. She played it very cool.

During our junior year, Wanda and I were assigned to the same homeroom. I smiled at her often, and she smiled back. But her overall manner was still chilly.

Then one day I saw her walking through the hallway by herself, and I got brave. I said, "Could I carry your books?" She smiled and replied, "Sure." And suddenly, the ice began to break.

A few weeks later, Oberlin High School announced its annual Sadie Hawkins dance. To my pleasant surprise—and elation—Wanda asked me to be her date. Later, she told me that the girl asking out the guy was not her idea of a "proper" date. But, she said, there were other girls in our homeroom class who had their eye on me, so she had to move quickly. We had a great time, and I discovered the beautiful Miss Young was also an excellent dancer.

After the Sadie Hawkins dance, we started dating regularly—and I did the asking. I walked her home from school whenever I could, and we talked about everything under the sun. The war that was raging in Europe cast a cloud of uncertainty over our world, but we both dreamed of a bright future. Wanda told me of her hopes of becoming an elementary school teacher. I filled her in on my plan of becoming a world-famous jazz musician.

"YOU'RE THE ONE"

As Mr. Young's depression grew deeper, Alden became Wanda's primary guardian and caregiver. He took his responsibility quite seriously. He made sure she completed her homework, was in the house before dark, and was in church every Sunday—whether she wanted to go or not. His strictness was especially evident when it came to my relationship with his sister.

One afternoon, I asked Wanda if she would come hear me play at another school's dance the next evening. At first, Wanda didn't seem interested. Then she told me she would like to go but that her brother probably would never allow her to go someplace where she would have to spend most of the evening sitting alone.

Alden actually surprised us. He agreed to let Wanda go. But there was one condition: He would go with us. Wanda was horrified at the thought of her twenty-nine-year-old brother acting as a chaperon, but she assented. It turned out to be the first of many "dates" where Alden, without complaint, sat with Wanda while I performed with my band. Years later, Wanda realized just how special her brother's efforts were.

A year flew by, and Wanda and I were getting more and more serious. One evening, I was invited to play a solo for a musical program at the Methodist Church, and Wanda attended with me. I was dressed to the nines in a new Rust-checkered suit and vest. And I stood up there and played a jazzy arrangement of "I Must Tell Jesus" with our piano player Frank Williams accompanying. Wanda sat there in the front pew, watching me with those lovely brown eyes. After the program, she congratulated me and told me how proud she was of me. Then she said, "You know, while I was watching you play and hearing you, I realized that you're the boy for my life."

Oh, man, did that ever feel good to hear! I hugged her tightly and—for the first time—gave her a big kiss.

THE OTHER MAN

A few weeks into our senior year of high school, my jazz orchestra traveled to Mansfield, Ohio, for one of our biggest engagements yet. It was a tremendous dance that drew hundreds of folks.

When I got home, I looked forward to seeing Wanda and telling her all about our big weekend. But Wanda had news of her own.

Before I could dial her number, Wanda called me. Her sweet voice was filled with added enthusiasm as she welcomed me home. She said, "Howard, come over here right away. I've got some exciting news to tell you!"

I made my way to her house as quickly as I could. I greeted a young woman who was bursting with joy. I'd never seen her so happy. I said to myself, *I hope she didn't meet a new dude while I was out of town*. Turns out, she did meet Someone.

"Let me tell you what happened to me," she said. "While you were away, four guys came to our church from Biola Institute in Los Angeles. Two were trumpeters, one was a trombone player, and the other a pianist. And they were going across the country in this old Model-T Ford. And they happened to stop by Oberlin, and the pastor invited them to come to our church to lead a youth revival meeting."

Wanda was a member of an integrated Christian and Missionary Alliance (C&MA) congregation, where her sister Ruth played piano. Her pastor, Miss Elsie Gatherer, was a bit of an anomaly in the C&MA. She was a Nazarene preacher from Scotland. She had come to Oberlin years ago as an itinerant preacher. But her passionate expository preaching was so profound and effective that the local C&MA asked her to stay on as the Oberlin church's pastor, much to the chagrin of national denominational leaders, who disapproved of women preachers. But Miss Gatherer's ministry was so Christ centered it was difficult to dismiss her.

Wanda explained that Miss Gatherer had asked the traveling Biola students to play their music and deliver their testimonies to the congregation full of teenagers. Their joyful music expressed their love for Jesus, Wanda said. And then the young men spoke about how God had brought strength and peace into their lives despite heartaches and personal losses. This resonated with Wanda, who had, in effect, lost both her parents when her mother died. As the students continued to share their hearts through words and music, it became clear to Wanda that they were for real. These young men were determined to give Jesus their all, because He had given His all—His life—for them.

Suddenly the personal pain and bitterness Wanda had hidden in her heart began to melt away, and she realized what she had been missing all those years since her mother's death. "Howard," she said, "last night I went forward and gave my heart completely to Jesus Christ."

I went to the all-Negro Mount Zion Baptist, and Wanda went to the Oberlin Alliance Church. Wanda occasionally joined me at Mount Zion, where we would sing together in the youth choir. As far as I was concerned, we were both good Christians. But Wanda's news seemed to signal something greater. Though our relationship had been getting serious, we had never really discussed our religious lives. Now it seemed to be coming to the fore in a major way, and I didn't know what to think.

Although I didn't understand it, I was glad for Wanda's testimony of her born-again experience. After all, I told myself, a little religion never hurt anyone. I had mine, and now she had hers. But it wasn't long before I found that Wanda had something more than just mere religion.

THE ULTIMATUM

A few days after Wanda's announcement, I asked her to go to the movies with me. She refused to go. This was odd! Wanda and I had always enjoyed going to the movies together. Something wasn't right.

But my greatest surprise came when I asked her to go

dancing with me. She had always been a wonderful dancer and enjoyed it as much as I did. But again she turned me down. This new Wanda troubled me. She was no longer interested in the fun things we had always done together, or even in my work as a jazz musician.

Slowly I became convinced that our lives were now completely different. We had nothing in common anymore. We were living in two different worlds. I didn't know it then, but Wanda's conversion proved to be a mighty tool in the hand of God to eradicate all my illusions about the place and purpose of God in our lives.

Seeing Wanda's consistent Christian living challenged me to rethink my own religious experience. I had gone forward to join the church at Mount Zion Baptist. But it wasn't revolutionizing. It was something I did and then put away in a compartment. I had gotten baptized, then went out to perform at a nightclub. In my mind, there was your religious life and your real life, and the two needed to meet only on Sunday mornings.

But now Wanda, the love of my life, was joining the two parts together all the time, seven days a week. What did this mean for our future?

Wanda convinced me to attend her church from time to time. Soon, I began to recognize a difference between the teaching at my church and the Bible-centered preaching delivered to her congregation.

Today I look back at a lot of the preachers we had at Mount Zion, and I realize many of them graduated from Oberlin Theological Seminary, which years ago was a good school, but by the 1920s and 1930s, it had become liberal. (Years later, Oberlin's seminary closed its doors and merged

with Vanderbilt Seminary in Nashville.) With a few exceptions, the young Oberlin graduates who came to our church
to preach always brought a message heavy on philosophy, but
never the gospel. In fact, I didn't know what the gospel was.
(Of course, there were several outstanding preachers such as
Gardner Taylor, James Earl Massey, and Leon Troy, who have
gone on to touch many lives with the gospel.)

I always admired the dynamism of those preachers. Even as
a kid growing up, if I saw a man who could preach, I was fascinated. And I remember times I locked myself in my bedroom with a Bible and mimicked preachers in front of my
mirror. But, alas, most of the preaching I received was full of
soaring oratory but lacking when it came to the basic message of salvation through Jesus Christ.

However, this was not the case when I went to Wanda's
church. Whether it was Miss Gatherer or some other preacher, each time I went, I got the gospel. Unfortunately, I wasn't
ready to make the kind of commitment it seemed to demand.

Before Wanda's conversion, we had talked often about getting married someday. We dreamed of going to college together—her to study education, me to study music. I used to
tell her, "I'm going to hit the big time, and I'll buy you fur
coats and expensive jewelry. We'll travel the world." And she
liked that. But now that she had experienced this transformation, my hopes of making her my wife seemed to be getting slimmer and dimmer.

One night after church, it all came to a head. Wanda, I suppose, had grown weary of my "not getting it." And I had
grown tired of not having my old girlfriend. We walked
slowly to her house, where we eventually sat together on her
porch swing. We sat in silence for several minutes. Then final-

ly her soft, gentle hands took hold of mine, and she explained to me that unless I gave my heart to Christ, she would have to stop seeing me.

Wanda's words cut deep, yet I wasn't willing or ready to change my ways. Losing her was the last thing on earth I wanted to happen, but I didn't have the strength or desire to become something that I wasn't.

"Wanda," I said, "our difference of ideas on spiritual matters doesn't have to come between us or separate us. I love you, Wanda. And more than anything else in the world, I want to marry you. I'll be a great bandleader someday, making lots of money. You'll never want for anything."

Wanda took a deep breath, and then I heard her say those most disturbing words: "Howard, even though I love you, I love Christ more. Therefore, unless you accept Jesus Christ as your personal Savior, I will not be able to see you anymore, because we'll have nothing more in common with each other."

I was crushed. How do you respond to something like that? She went on to tell me that I should consider giving up my glamorous dreams of superstardom, because there is more to life than fame and fortune. "It is my personal conviction, now that I'm a Christian, that God has something better for you in life than a career as a sax player," she said. "I am going to pray, and our church is praying, that someday soon you'll give your heart and life to Jesus, and then use your talents to serve the Lord."

She let go of my hand and stood to her feet. I could see the tears welling up in her eyes. Yet she seemed determined to stand firm. "Howard, you keep playing, and I'll keep praying."

And with that, she said good-bye.

FOUR

Strong Prayers *and* Naysayers

DECIDING TO FOLLOW JESUS

I t's not easy being in competition with Jesus. At times you may think you've got a shot, but eventually He always has the upper hand. When Wanda chose Him over me, I recognized my disadvantage. I realized how deep Wanda's religious commitment went, and I honestly respected that. That didn't mean I liked it.

There was no way to describe the feelings that went through me the night Wanda ended our relationship. I was angry, brokenhearted, and as miserable as I'd ever felt in my life. Her final words that night spoiled everything for me. Once and for all she had declared her terms for my continued friendship with her. And for me, those terms were too high.

I couldn't live up to them. And I didn't want to. As much as I loved Wanda Young, I still believed in my heart that jazz music had to be the top priority in my life, and Wanda was a close second.

Although I could not share Wanda's conviction, our talk that night only deepened my respect for her. Her devotion to God and the Bible seemed unshakable. Nothing could sway her loyalty, not even the thought of losing me. I hated to admit it, but I knew she would be completely satisfied with Christ—with or without me.

I avoided all contact with Wanda. When I saw her at school, I went the other way. Too stubborn and proud to give in, I told myself I could live without Wanda and her Jesus. I resolved to lose myself in my music and the pleasures of the world. I knew my dance band, the money, success, and praises of our fans would be enough to dull the pain of a lost girl-friend.

But as the days trudged on, the pain in my heart seemed only to intensify. The more I tried to find contentment from the world, the more I realized I was only fooling myself. I was miserable in mind and soul. The conviction of my wrongness and guilt before God grew worse. I became more and more restless and wretched, dissatisfied with everything the world had to offer.

Worst of all, my unhappiness began to affect my music. I couldn't play as I used to. The men in the band noticed it. I knew it wouldn't be long before audiences would know it too. My colleagues were puzzled. No one knew better than they how much I had loved my sax and clarinet and the music I created with them. Actually, I couldn't understand it myself.

Suddenly the music of the band did not grip and charm me as it once had. I didn't look forward to playing for big, special dances. The wonderful, spine-tingling feeling that once thrilled me as we poured out the big band sounds was gone. I realized at last, to my own dismay, that I no longer played because I loved it, but because it was my job and the only work I wanted to do.

My music, it turned out, was not the biggest thing in my life after all. Without Wanda and without peace in my heart, my music was empty—it was nothing at all.

FROM CRISIS TO FAITH

After two weeks of sheer misery, I had enough. I couldn't run away anymore—from Wanda, or from her God.

One Sunday night, in my despair, I decided to visit Wanda's church again. Spotting her near the front of the sanctuary, I slipped into the pew across from her. After a few moments, I saw Wanda look in my direction. She flashed a precious smile. I could tell she was happy to see me, but it didn't change our state of affairs. I was still hurting.

When Miss Gatherer took to the pulpit, I'm sure she recognized me as Wanda's ex-boyfriend—*the one we've all been praying for.* But her expression never let on to this fact. Her sermon, however, seemed tailored especially for me. It contrasted the world's riches with the true wealth found in Christ.

"You think you'll be losing if you follow Christ," she said, "but Jesus is a giver and not a taker. He wants to give you even more than what you dream of. And His first gift is peace—peace that you've settled your account with God. His next gift is joy—joy that no matter what the future holds, He can be trusted!"

Miss Gatherer had my attention. Suddenly, everything she

was saying made sense. I was a sinner before a holy God. My life had been spent trying to make myself happy, but now I understood true happiness could come only from surrendering myself to Christ and allowing Him to have His way with me.

When the invitation hymn started to play, I had no doubt about what I needed to do. I stood and headed to the altar; there I quietly met my Lord and Savior. The congregation wasn't quiet, though. They began to shout hallelujahs and praises of gratitude to God.

As I fell to my knees at the altar, Wanda, Miss Gatherer, and the other two hundred congregants knelt in prayer for me. On my knees, I poured out my heart to God in tears and repentance. I confessed my sins and begged for forgiveness.

That night God answered my prayer—and Wanda's prayer. He saved me. I stood up and testified that I was saved by faith in Christ. I was conscious that I was a true child of God. I felt good in my heart. My mind was at rest. And for the first time in my life, I knew that somewhere, somehow, God had something for me to do for Him. Wanda grabbed me and hugged me for a long time. She was crying. And the people around us were saying, "Thank God, that Jones boy got saved!"

Everyone was elated, and I was feeling pretty good. Then Miss Gatherer approached me. "All right," she said. "Two Sundays from now, you're going to preach to the young people."

"I can't preach," I said incredulously. "I play music."

"Well, you've got to share your testimony," she said. And as far as she was concerned, the appointment was set in stone. Her philosophy was, *you get saved, you go to work for the Lord*. There was no space in-between—that way the devil doesn't have a chance to interrupt your flow.

So, two weeks later I was in the pulpit with an open Bible, sharing my journey to faith in God. I have no idea what I said that evening, but I recall I was extremely happy when it was over. However, at the same time, I recall feeling God nudge at my heart a little as I was speaking to the congregation.

From the night of my conversion on, things began to happen. I threw away my cigarettes and gave up the smoking habit that I had picked up a few years earlier when I became a hotshot musician. Drinking, dancing, and other carnal pleasures became things of the past for me. Preaching and studying God's Word began to take on a new fascination in my mind. I was a changed person. But there was one great battle that remained to be fought between the Lord and me.

YOU GOTTA SERVE SOMEBODY

The Lord made it clear to me at that time that, as a Christian, I had to give up my band and surrender my future fully to Him. I was already convinced I would never be happy with music alone. But now that I was a Christian, I still hoped secretly that I could have Christ, Wanda, and the dance orchestra. I knew in my heart that I was wrong, but I fought the Lord for it anyway.

God, it seemed, was putting His hand on the lingering idol in my life—the orchestra itself. The thought of giving it up was pure torture. Outwardly, I told God I would do it, hoping that saying it would be enough. But I was just saying words with my mouth. I didn't mean it at all. God knew I didn't mean it, and He began to deal with me in a way I shall never forget.

It was during the biggest dance event of the season. Duke

Ellington's The International Sweethearts of Rhythm, an all-female orchestra that was one of the most famous of the day, was the featured band at this popular nightclub, Crystal Beach, on Lake Erie. All my old friends were going, and I knew every member from our orchestra would be there. No jazz fan was going to miss this night of nights. If ever I felt the power of Satan tempting me to do something, it was then.

I had no doubt that God was against it, and I knew what Wanda thought about it. She was away visiting relatives in another city, but before she left she had written me a letter begging me not to go to that dance. She said it would ruin my testimony as a new Christian.

The battle raged in my soul. I had to make a decision. Finally, I decided on what I thought would be a good solution—a compromise. I would go to the dance, but only to drive Clarence and his girlfriend there. I would not go into the dance hall itself, I vowed; I would only stand outside and listen to the music.

When we arrived at the nightclub, my brother and his girlfriend went in to the dance. I stayed around outside the ballroom and for a while had a good time talking with some of my friends. But soon, someone asked about my recent acceptance of Christ. It seemed nearly everyone there had heard about it. Even a couple of my orchestra friends talked with me about my conversion experience.

"Howard, now that you're a Christian, are you going to leave the band?" one friend asked.

"Yes," I replied. "I do feel God wants me to leave the band. At times I even feel as though God wants me to preach the gospel. But as to when I'm going to leave the band, I am not prepared to say right now."

Soon crowds of laughing people began coming from the dance hall for a break in between concert sets. My brother saw me and came to where I was standing.

"Howard, it's a wonderful dance," Clarence said. "Why don't you come in? You don't have to dance, you know. Here is half of my ticket. Come on in and hear the Duke, man."

Something pulled hard inside of me, but I shook my head. "No, I don't think I will," I said. "It just wouldn't feel right."

But after Clarence left, I began to reason with myself. *It wouldn't be a sin if I just went in and listened to the music—as long as I kept my promise not to do any dancing.*

All the while I argued with myself, I moved closer and closer to the door of the club, drawn as if by a gigantic magnet to the bright lights and the jazz music. With each step I took, I could hear two voices, clear and distinct, in the depths of my soul. I could hear the voice of Satan telling me not to restrict myself—that there was nothing wrong or sinful in what I was going to do. But I also heard the voice of God telling me I must not go into the dance hall.

The sin, I knew, was not a matter of going into the club, or even dancing. None of those things is sinful in and of themselves. The sin would be in failing to die to my own powerful desire to find fulfillment from the world. Perhaps one day down the line, going into a secular dance hall would not be an issue. But right now, it was something God did not want me to do.

But I kept on walking. I knew what God had said was right, but too stubborn and set in my foolish ways to obey, I listened to the devil and went into the dance hall.

When I got inside, I did not experience the secret thrill that I had hoped for. The music of the band did not excite me as it once had. Instead, I felt a strange, depressing feeling of deep conviction. It was the conviction of sin, I knew, brought on by the power of the Holy Spirit. It was so heavy that I felt it would crush the life out of me.

Beads of perspiration stood out on my forehead. My heart pounded as though I had just run a race. I began trembling all over. I walked slowly to the bar and ordered a cold orange soda, thinking it would steady me—and let onlookers know that I was not drinking beer or liquor. Some of my own band members noticed me and were watching my strange actions.

"Howard, are you sick?" one friend asked.

"No, I'm not sick," I answered. "I'll be OK in a minute."

THE CALL OF A PREACHER

All the while I was in the ballroom, the orchestra was playing, but I don't think I heard a note of the music. I was so deeply convicted of my wrongheaded condition before the Lord that all I could hear was my own heart thumping in my ears. I felt like a criminal condemned to death. I was sure everyone was staring at me.

I started to panic. "I've got to get out of here—fast!" I told myself. Turning quickly from the bar, I walked as fast as I could to the nearest exit. "If I don't get out of here right now, I'll die," I said.

I rushed through the door and pushed my way through the crowd and across the outer porch until I was finally on the ground outside. The clean, cool night air swept over me. Tears of shame streamed down my face as I looked up into the beautiful moon-lit sky and on the shimmering waves of

Lake Erie cried out to God from the depths of my soul:

Oh, God! If You will forgive my sins this night, and my disobedi-ence, I will serve You the rest of my life. Lord, I know You want me to leave the band and surrender my life to You. Tonight, Lord, if You will help me, I will leave the orchestra and accept Your call to preach the gospel of Jesus Christ.

God heard my prayer. He answered it by lifting the weight of conviction and guilt. Then He flooded my soul with peace and joy such as I had never known before.

The next day, I hurried to Wanda's house to tell her my news. From the wide grin on my face, she immediately knew that something wonderful had happened.

"Wanda," I said laughing, as I entered her house. "God wants me to be a preacher."

Wanda was speechless. She stood there staring at me with this profoundly blank look on her face.

"What's wrong?" I asked. "Don't you want to be a preach-er's wife?"

With that, her face began to soften and take on the more recognizable expression of joy and excitement. She threw her arms around me and laughed. "I knew God had some-thing special for you to do," she said.

I proceeded to tell her the whole story of my experience at the nightclub the previous night. I told her how I had tried to enjoy myself at the dance, but how I just couldn't shake the sense that I was going against the Spirit of God. And then I tried to describe that supernatural moment when I con-ceded total control to the Lord and freely embraced His new call on my life.

Wanda was thrilled, but many of my friends fell emphati-cally in the other category—especially after I made the an-

nouncement that I was leaving the band. Their reactions
sounded like a chorus of negativity:

"What?" they said. "You're crazy to leave the orchestra."

"Howard, you've gone mad! You could become a famous
sax player some day, man. What's wrong with you?"

"Those religious feelings will go away after a while, man.
Just wait and see."

"Jazz is in your life. It's in your blood. You will be back in
the orchestra in two weeks."

On and on it went, but my confidence in the Lord's call on
my life brought me the courage to endure the opposition
with grace. It was not easy though. Many nights I wet my
pillow with tears. The trials and testing were as great as any I
had ever known. But God stood by me and gave me the
strength and wisdom to go on with Him and withstand the
peer pressures of my unbelieving friends.

Perhaps my greatest challenge was related to my health.
After I left the band, I was suddenly sicker than I had ever
been in my life. Playing long hours for dances and running
day and night with the old crowd had broken me physically. I
suffered strange fainting spells and serious attacks of indigestion. In bed at night, I felt as though I was sinking through
the floor. Attacks of indigestion were so bad, I was sure I was
going to die.

Finally, I went to see a doctor. He told me I had high
blood pressure. Though I was a young man, he said my blood
pressure was that of a 65-year-old. As if that were not
enough, the doctor warned me that my condition was so serious that even if I did live to be 30 years old, I would be a
complete physical wreck. My indigestion, he said, was
caused by nervous disorders. This began a long period of

rest, diet, and medical treatment for my recovery.

One evening an attack of indigestion was so painful that I could do nothing but go to bed. As I lay there in agony, I began to pray. I told the Lord that I knew I was saved, but I still was not sure if He really wanted me to preach the gospel. I was willing, but I did not see how I could serve Him with such a sick body. I asked Him to heal my body and deliver me from my misery so that I might serve Him well.

After praying, I fell into a deep sleep. As I slept, the Lord gave me an amazing vision. I saw myself standing in the pulpit of a very large church. The building was crowded with people. It seemed as though I were conducting a great service. With arms outstretched, I invited the people to come to Christ. They came down to the church altar from every direction. Many were weeping! God was there in our midst, as men and women found Christ as their Savior. Wanda was there, too, kneeling near me, praying for souls to come to Christ. It was morning when I woke. To my astonishment, as I got out of bed, I felt strong and refreshed as never before. Then and there I knew with unshakable assurance that God had called me to the Christian ministry and that He would completely heal my sick body. In time, He did just that.

When Wanda and I told Miss Gatherer about my decision to become a preacher, she clasped her hands together in delight. "Both of you have so much talent that I just know the Lord has a special place for you."

With her encouragement, we began to pray about attending the same Bible school as Wanda's sister Ruth—Nyack, a Christian and Missionary Alliance college in metropolitan New York. This school was noted for its emphasis on missions. There was one problem: Like my nay-saying friends, my dad thought I was idiotic to give up my future in music for some elusive call to ministry. And he was bent on making it a difficult path for me to tread.

But by now, both Wanda and I were so confident of our destiny together that we viewed each episode of adversity not as an insurmountable obstacle but as a momentary bump in the narrow road—and an opportunity to trust God more.

PART TWO

The Education of a Preacher

FIVE

Go East, Young Man
PREPARATION ON THE MOUNT OF NYACK

Wanda and I decided it would be best to wait until after we completed our schooling to get married. And so the summer of 1941 was spent preparing mentally, spiritually, and financially for our big move to Nyack, New York, in the fall.

The decision to attend the three-year program at Nyack was not without its challenges. As I mentioned earlier, my dad was not keen on the idea of me tossing out my musical aspirations in favor of going to a tiny Bible school. A lifelong Baptist (by pedigree, if not faith), Dad was leery of Miss Gatherer, the C&MA denomination, and its predominantly white heritage.

"Whoever heard of The Christian and Missionary Alliance, anyway?" he told me when I started attending Wanda's church. "Sounds like Christian Science or something. But if you want to go over there and follow that white preacher-woman, you can."

Though I expected some flak, I was taken aback by the ferocity of Dad's reaction to my Nyack decision. His cutting words left me scrambling to defend what I knew in my heart was God's will for my future.

In some ways, I could understand his resentment. My dad was a good man who had poured his hopes and dreams into raising Clarence and me with a passionate appreciation of music. When I decided to quit the band, Dad felt personally betrayed because he'd spent a lot of money on my musical education. Later when I told him about my new call to ministry and to Nyack, he couldn't stand it anymore. He questioned my discernment and, I think, wondered whether I was just trying to please Wanda.

"I don't understand you," Dad said. "You want to be a preacher, that's all right. But why don't you go to Oberlin or some school that's better known?"

"No, Dad. I know the Lord is leading me to Nyack to study the Bible, and that's where I want to go." It was probably one of the first times in my life that I actually stood firm against my dad's wishes. "I have to follow God's plan," I told him.

"God's plan? I'll tell you what God's plan is. He's planning for you to be a somebody. You're not going to amount to anything going to that school. You're throwing your life away, and I'm not going to help you do that. Don't expect one cent from me."

His remarks stung deeply, but I knew it wasn't a matter of simply changing my mind. This was God's business now, and I was certain He would take care of me. After a long, uncomfortable silence, I finally said, "That's OK, Dad. I'll trust the Lord."

Mother, of course, could read the pain and sadness I was trying to conceal. Later that day, she put her arm around me and said, "Son, don't let your father discourage you. I'm proud of what you're doing. Just give your dad time to cool down."

And then she said the words that let me know it was all going to work out. "Even if your father doesn't come around, the Lord is going to honor your determination to prepare for whatever He wants you to do. I'll try to help you when I can, but just know you are doing the right thing."

A NEW WORLD

Back in those days before there was a Pennsylvania Turnpike, it took forever to travel east. But a gracious friend from Cleveland volunteered to drive Wanda and me the five hundred miles from Oberlin to Nyack. We arrived at the campus just before midnight and were immediately impressed by the spectacular view of the massive gray buildings spread out on a large hill overlooking the grand Hudson River. The moonbeams glistened on the water as we drove up, and several miles downstream we could see the warm lights from Sing Sing Prison glowing softly in the night sky. The spectacle of the place was truly overwhelming for two kids from northeast Ohio. Both Wanda and I felt we had suddenly entered a brave new, dreamlike world.

The Missionary Training Institute (which would later become Nyack College) was founded in 1882 by A. B. Simpson, one of the foremost figures in the American missionary movement during the nineteenth century and the key player in the formation of The Christian and Missionary Alliance Church.

The college president at that time was Dr. Thomas S. Mosley, a godly man who drilled students on the power of prayer with wonderfully quotable nuggets like, "Little prayer, little power. Much prayer, much power."

Knowing the missions emphasis of the school, Wanda and I walked onto that campus with the great feeling that our future was boundless. We would prepare ourselves to do whatever God had in store for us, and to go wherever in the world He pointed. In our naïve youth, we didn't think that most mission boards in the 1940s were more interested in sending out their own white missionaries rather than people of color. But we pressed forward with the idealism of fervent faith.

We soon discovered the severity of the many rules and restrictions imposed upon Nyack students. I had read about some of these strict guidelines before applying to the school, but I never imagined how suffocating those guidelines would feel once I experienced them off the page. There was no hand-holding allowed or public display of affection of any kind. There was a rotating schedule of assigned seating for meals, so Wanda and I got to sit near each other in the cafeteria only once every two weeks. What's more, we were allowed to go out on dates only once a week—and then it had to be with two other couples. This was enough to cramp the style of a happily courting couple. In fact, our romantic moments were dramatically curbed. Thankfully, we were allowed to sit together at the mandatory Friday night missionary meeting and during the Sunday evening services.

Though some of the rules seemed a bit overboard, we quickly adjusted and actually came to appreciate the limitations placed on us. It made the times we did have together all the more special and forced us to learn to communicate in new ways—whether in lengthy letters or quick glances across the room.

SECOND THOUGHTS

Way down at the bottom of the hill, away from where most of the school's facilities stood, was Wilson Dormitory, one of the male residence halls. The place was not much to speak of, with creaking stairs, poor lighting, and aging decor. When I first entered my small dorm room, I had a fleeting moment of regret—*What have I gotten myself into here?*—but then I began to meet my fellow students, experienced their disarming kindness, and began to trust God that I'd feel better about things in the morning.

The next day I discovered my roommate was a young man named Clarence Bowman. He was a black student from Oberlin who also had been saved under the preaching of Miss Gatherer. (In fact, four other future preachers, including myself, had been saved under the preaching of Miss Gatherer at Oberlin Alliance.) I was genuinely happy to see Clarence's familiar face amid my strange surroundings.

"They put me in here to look out after you," Bowman said smiling. A senior, he would be moving on to Gordon College in Massachusetts after graduating from Nyack.

"That's great," I said. So we fixed up that old room. My mother sent me some shades and curtains, and I had a guy come in and repair the floor. Soon the place was feeling less decrepit. In the days ahead, I would meet God there many times.

During my first week at Nyack, I received an airmail special delivery letter from Dad. He wrote to tell me that Stanley Austin, a close friend of mine, had been killed in an automobile accident. I was devastated, saddened that a young man my age could have his dreams cut short while I was a world away pursuing mine. My heart wept even more when it hit me that I wouldn't be able to attend the funeral. As I stood in the chapel hall, holding back tears as I processed the letter's tragic announcement, I felt a hand on my shoulder.

"You got some sad news?" a voice asked.

I turned to see four white students from my dorm. "Yes," I said. "A friend of mine back home was killed yesterday."

"May we pray for you and your friend's family?" asked Bob Heffer, a tall blond-haired fellow, who was the owner of that original voice of concern. He seemed to be the spokesman for this little group that also included Bill Frederick, Bob Gray, and Paul Troph.

I was almost speechless but managed to say, "Yes, yes. Thank you."

And there in the middle of the common area, those five young men gathered around me and prayed, one by one. It was one of many defining moments that God used to open my heart to my white brothers and sisters at Nyack, and my eyes to the meaning of the apostle Paul's statement in 1 Thessalonians: "Pray without ceasing." I had always wondered about the practicality of such an instruction. But at Nyack I saw students praying with each other on the spur of the moment, professors who opened each class with prayer and occasionally stopped classes midlecture to pray for distraught students, and young men and women who started and ended their days on their knees.

I gleaned the importance of developing a set time to study and reflect on God's Word. I learned how to preach before an audience of aspiring preachers (not an easy thing). I heard from missionary after missionary who told stories of journeying to the farthest reaches of the earth to share the Good

News of Christ's salvation. I saw the value of simply being available to help a grieving person cry. These were models that would inspire me to greater devotion and faith in every area of my life.

Later on in the week, I met three other black students on campus who shared my love for music: Herbert and Douglas Oliver, two brothers from Birmingham, Alabama; and Charles Williams from New Kensington, Pennsylvania. Somehow, we had all gathered around the Chapel Hall's piano one evening to sing some Negro spirituals and discovered that our voices in four-part harmony blended nicely. As a result, we ended up forming the Gospel Crusaders, an a cappella quartet that some said was the best music ensemble on campus. During the next three years, we sang at most of the big campus events and traveled to churches in Harlem, Pennsylvania, and throughout the region to perform. I had given up my dream of traveling the land with my jazz orchestra, but God had replaced it with a greater privilege—traveling the land to sing and promote His praises and preach His Word.

Many of the people who crossed my path at Nyack would go on to become dear friends with whom I've stayed in contact throughout the decades. Though it clearly was not a perfect place, I grew to understand and appreciate God's purposes for taking me there.

TRIPPING OVER RACE

I learned to take the good with the bad at Nyack. But sometimes it seemed that the bad was taking the upper hand.

In a student body of six hundred, Wanda and I were two of only twelve blacks. And among those other blacks were two

faces from Oberlin—my roommate Clarence Bowman and
Wanda's sister Ruth, both seniors. It was the 1940s and the
school had started opening its doors to Negroes only twenty
years before, so we still felt a lot like "test cases."

The white students, for the most part, were from the
South and were not accustomed to having blacks on campus.
Since most had never associated with blacks in their churches
or communities, many of them treated us rudely. We were
always conscious of their listening ears and watching eyes
evaluating our every word and step. Wanda and I were disappointed to find the same old prejudices and the same dis-
trusting stares on a Christian campus. Wanda used to tell of
the sadness she felt whenever a white male would open the
door for another white student but let it close in her face.

Then there were the uneasy questions raised about the
place of blacks in Christian service. Were we truly "all one in
Christ Jesus," as the apostle Paul had asserted to the Galatians,
or were there racially delineated "divisions of labor" in the
kingdom of God?

On Friday nights, we black students would listen as missionaries challenged the student body with the call of the
Great Commission—to "go into all the world, and preach
the gospel." But when one of us would raise the question
about blacks being sent to the mission field, we were given
many reasons why it wasn't advisable. For example, some
mission boards were concerned that black missionaries
would have children who would need to be educated in the
same schools as the white missionaries' children. Others said
the nationals—or "natives" as they were called then—
wouldn't accept the gospel from a black man but would
expect him to live "on their level."

I never bought into those shortsighted lines of reasoning. Clearly they were imposing worldly restrictions on God's activity in the world. It took many nights of angst-ridden prayers and of long discussions with other black students to help me keep the proper perspective: God was in the business of salvation and reconciliation, and He would use whomever and whatever He wanted to accomplish His purposes. No, God was not color-blind, as some well-meaning folks would tell me in later years; He made me black and that guy white and that fellow Asian for good reasons—reasons He may share with us someday (though I doubt we'll need to ask). However, He never intended race, class, or culture to become barriers to relationships among His people.

I like to think that, in a small way, our presence as black students on the Nyack campus helped enlighten the hearts and minds of many white students and professors. I certainly had to acknowledge and deal with many of my own subtle (and some not-so-subtle) prejudices.

WAR COMES HOME

Around the end of that first semester, our isolated little world was changed forever. I was in the recreation room at Wilson Hall, playing shuffleboard when word spread across the campus: Pearl Harbor had been bombed. The war that had been a European affair officially arrived in our country.

Everyone in the recreation room froze for a long moment before dropping their sticks and dashing to our dorm rooms to gather around our radios. We anxiously took in the details of the attack as we wondered what this would mean for our future.

On the morning of September 11, 2001, I remember
flashing back to that dark December day in 1941. Many news
commentators compared the 9/11 terrorist attacks on our
country to the Pearl Harbor tragedy, and I agree that it had
that same unsettling effect. Of course, back in 1941, I had the
added anxiety of wondering how long it would be before
they "called my number" to join the fray overseas.

Many male students were eager to enlist immediately.
Nyack's administrators, however, recommended that we all
stay in school until we were drafted. They reasoned that the
world would now need trained Christian leaders more than
ever. Many of us were persuaded to stay (myself included),
but others left to defend their country.

I would learn later that since I had completed at least half
of a semester in a theological school, I was exempt from the
draft. Though I had been prepared to "answer the call" if it
were sounded to me, I was honestly relieved that I would not
be required to enlist in the military. If I had gone, I would
have wanted to join a chaplaincy program. But I had heard
many despairing stories about how most black recruits were
generally consigned to menial jobs that would free up the
white soldiers for "more important" work, so I was nervous
that I might get lost in that shuffle of segregation if I were
called to serve.

My brother Clarence enlisted in the army some months
after Pearl Harbor, so I was continually on my knees on his
behalf. Fortunately, as a member of the army band, he was not
in line for combat duty. Wanda's brother Louis Young, however, did see combat. An army enlistee, Louis (L.C.) had also
joined after Pearl Harbor.

One learns to live with the disconcerting knowledge that a

loved one serving in the midst of a world war could be killed at any moment, and Wanda did an admirable job of giving her anxieties to God in prayer. But one afternoon during our sophomore year, Wanda received that telephone call from home that everybody dreaded in those days. It was Ruth calling to inform her that L. C. had been killed in North Africa.

Wanda, of course, was devastated. In fact, she had just received a letter from him a few days earlier. We prayed tearful prayers that day. The other students and I did our best to console Wanda. But it would be the kind of heartrending sorrow that only time and prayer could heal.

SIX

Ready, Set, Grow
LIVING, LOVING, AND LEARNING

I officially proposed to Wanda in July 1943, the summer following our sophomore year. I had secured summer employment at an Oberlin foundry, cleaning excess metal from huge, freshly fired castings. It was strenuous work, and by the conclusion of each day, my lanky frame was covered in layers of stinky soot. I saved the money earned from that grimy job to purchase an engagement ring for my fiancée.

Wanda and I traveled to a jewelry store in nearby Lorain, Ohio, to pick out the ring. She fell in love with a beautiful half-carat diamond solitaire that cost me $150—big bucks in that day.

The semesters following our freshmen year at Nyack proved to be heady times. I continued to be amazed at the wonderful commitment to prayer I saw in many of my professors and classmates. Both Wanda and I were repeatedly challenged to take our personal growth to new levels and trust God more in every part of our lives.

In addition to my role with the Gospel Crusaders quartet, I put my musical skills to use in the school orchestra. Both Wanda and I participated in the choir. There were numerous ministry opportunities. A white classmate and I played our saxophones many Sunday afternoons at a jail in nearby New City, New York. The Gospel Crusaders got invitations to perform throughout the New York area. I even started to do a little preaching in addition to singing.

I remember one great meeting we had in Harlem at Mother A.M.E. Zion Church whose pastor Benjamin Robeson, was the brother of the now-legendary singer and activist Paul Robeson. I sang with the quartet and preached a simple gospel message, challenging youths in the church to live their lives as if Christ were right there next to them all the time— because He was. When I gave the invitation, I figured we'd let the organist play for a minute or so and then sit down. But right away almost all the young people rose from their seats and came down front to commit their lives to Christ.

On another occasion, we sang at Sing Sing Prison. Before the service started, the inmates were passing out hymnbooks, and they said to us, "Praise the Lord, brothers. We're so glad you could be here."

I asked one older man, "Where did you find the Lord?"

"Right here in the prison," he said proudly. "I'm a free man on the inside."

So we sang, and I preached. And once again people came forward during the invitation. As I prayed with the inmates to receive Jesus, my skin filled with goose bumps, and I was overcome by the presence of God's Holy Spirit. Though I was excited to see people responding to my preaching, I realized immediately my meager efforts were not enough to bring about such outcomes. God was in the house, and He was teaching me in large and small ways how to get out of the way and let Him work.

PUTTING ME ON THE ALTAR

I told you God was constantly stretching Wanda and me, taking us to new levels of spiritual maturity. Perhaps one of the greatest—and most nerve-racking—tests of our commitment to God and to each other came early in our third year during what was known as Spiritual Emphasis Week.

The guest speakers were Reverend and Mrs. Gordon Wishart, a wise and insightful missionary couple. They delivered several talks on the practical aspects of ministry, especially about the relationship between husbands and wives. Since Wanda and I were eagerly looking forward to getting married after graduation, our ears perked up.

For many of the sessions, the speakers divided the student body into male and female groups. Reverend Wishart met with the men, and Mrs. Wishart spent time with the women. Separately and as a team, the Wisharts encouraged us to base all our actions on a solid, biblical foundation.

On the final night of the series, the Wisharts gave us a startling challenge: "You may be a Christian, but that doesn't necessarily mean that God wants you to be together," Mrs. Wishart declared boldly. "Don't assume you're doing the right thing; ask God to make sure you are! You may need to put your relationship on the altar until God tells you it's what He wants for you."

It was a provocative message, and it forced me to think hard about my relationship with Wanda. But, in fact, it didn't take me long to know in my heart and mind that I was on the right track. I loved Wanda. We had been through so much during our five years of dating. She was the woman God had brought into my life. And, by golly, I had no doubts about that whatsoever.

For Wanda, on the other hand, it was a different story. After the service, as I walked her to her dorm (it was permitted that night), I could tell she was feeling troubled by Mrs. Wishart's challenge. Her silence suggested something big was coming. "Have we taken our relationship for granted?" she finally said. "Have we really stopped and asked the Lord if our relationship is exactly what He wants? I don't know if I've really put you on the altar."

Oh, brother! Those were the words I didn't want to hear but that I knew were coming.

I found myself in a tricky position. On the one hand, I did not want to discount the importance of what the Wisharts had said and, in doing so, look less than spiritual. However, on the other hand, I saw no reason to put my beloved fiancée on the altar and risk losing her. Besides, I had just bought her a gorgeous diamond ring! (I admit my reasoning was a little on the selfish side at this stage, but I was a young man in love.) I wanted to tell Wanda not to take the Wisharts' words too literally, but I could see this was a serious issue for her. What's more, I admired her willingness to trust God completely for our future. So I held my tongue and put my faith in God. After all, if our relationship was built on a solid foundation, God would honor our faith just as He had honored Abraham's when the man obeyed God and placed his own son on the altar at Mount Moriah. Was I ready to trust God with that level of faith?

Wanda gave me back the engagement ring. And the two of us agreed to take some time to pray about our future together and to determine whether it was truly God's will.

It was an incredibly difficult period of waiting. I talked to my friend Bob Heffer about it, and he said he had gone through the same thing with his fiancée the year before. He told me to be patient. We laughed. And then we prayed.

A week passed—I believe the longest week of my life—and finally one day I saw Wanda coming down a hallway. She had a big smile on her face, which made me feel a little better. But I still wasn't sure what she had discovered. I flashed a curious grin and said, "Well, it's been a week. Any verdict yet?"

Wanda nodded and said, "You're the one!"

A lot of engagement rings and promise pins went back and forth that week. I was just thankful that I got to put the ring I had in my pocket back on the finger where it belonged.

PREACHING TO THE TREES

With the passage of time—and several homiletics exams—I could feel myself becoming a more proficient preacher. I loved to share the gospel. I loved to see men and women, boys and girls, and everyone in between moved to action and reaction by the proclamation of the Living Word of God. Early on, I could see the power that resides in God's Word. As I grew as a communicator of God's truth, I gained a new appreciation for that inimitable passage in Hebrews 4:12: "For the word of God is living and active. Sharper than any double-edged sword, it penetrates even to dividing soul and spirit, joints and marrow; it judges the thoughts and attitudes of the heart."

That kind of power was not to be handled lightly. And so, on those nights before I was to speak at a church service or some other function, I found myself spending increasing amounts of time on my knees before God, seeking wisdom and guidance for the enormous responsibility of presenting His message to needy hearts.

At Nyack, we were taught that the supreme task of the church is evangelism and that you never catch the true thrill of evangelism until you go to the fields abroad. We were taught that the central thrust of preaching is the message of the Cross, and that you can do it only through the anointing of the Holy Spirit. We were regularly drilled on the elements of good expository preaching. We were inculcated with sermons and studies by such greats as G. Campbell Morgan, F. B. Meyer, Andrew Murray, and of course, the "Prince of Preachers" Charles Spurgeon. Then there were the works of C&MA founder A. B. Simpson. His message on The Fourfold Gospel was especially hammered into us: A true and complete gospel must always give attention to Christ our Savior, Christ our Sanctifier, Christ our Healer, and Christ our Soon Coming King. Every Nyack student knew those four points inside and out.

I eventually discovered my preaching was most effective when it took an extemporaneous approach. As usual, I learned this the hard way. At the end of their second year, homiletics students were required to get up in front of their peers and preach for Professor Gilbert Johnson's class. That sermon constituted the final exam. I had learned to put my nerves in check when speaking at churches and other places, but this was different. I would actually receive a *grade* for this sermon. What's more, I would be the first student to speak!

The night before the exam, I was feeling a bit apprehensive. Wanda told me that she'd be praying for me, so that put me at ease a little. But I still could feel butterflies dive-bombing in my gut. Bob Heffer came into my room and asked if I was working on my message.

"Yes," I told him.

He looked at my notebook and flashed a slightly puzzled look. "Do you have it all typed out?"

"No. I don't preach that way. I just put an outline together," I explained.

"Howard, you should consider writing it all out," Bob said. "That way, you'll have a sufficient safety cushion."

Now I was beginning to worry. Was I preparing the right way? Would I blank out before the class and not be able to regroup using just an outline? Maybe I did need to write it all out. I began to doubt everything I knew to be true about my preaching style.

After Bob left, I stared at my outline for a long while. Then I relented; I typed out the whole sermon.

Big mistake! The next morning, I stood in front of the class and began to read my sermon. Almost immediately, I began to lose my train of thought. I eventually recovered, but the damage had been done. When I sat down, I knew I had fallen short of my usual effort. And my grade reflected it.

Later when I told Wanda, she was not interested in extending any cheap sympathy that day.

"It serves you right," she declared. "You know you're a good preacher. You never use a lot of notes. That's not your way. You have to trust your instincts—and trust God!"

Wanda, who would become an excellent speaker herself, was always encouraging me to greater heights. But she had never been afraid to tell me the truth either. And once again, she hammered it home.

A year later, in the senior level of Professor Johnson's homiletics course, I knew I had to redeem myself. The night before the big preaching exam, I gathered up my outline and went into a wooded area of the campus. I made sure nobody was around, and then I prayed out loud, "Alright Lord, You've got to help me with this one." And finally, I began to preach my sermon to the trees. I must have been summoning all my rage from messing up the previous year, because I really let the trees have it. When I was done, I knew those trees were saved—and I knew I was ready for the exam.

The next morning, my congregation was a professor and students, not a forest. Still, I managed to preach with that same fury I had unleashed on nature the night before. There were no missteps this time. I had exchanged my feeble anxiety for focused passion, and God honored it.

Years later, Professor Johnson came to hear me preach at an evangelistic meeting at Shell Point Village, in Fort Myers, Florida. After the service, I was able to share with him how grateful I was for having had the experience of participating in his classes. And he told me how proud he was of my achievements.

Effective preachers, I have learned, never lose their hunger for honing their craft. Nyack was really the place where I first developed that "appetite." I've been trying to feed it ever since.

SEVEN

Free *at Last*

THE FRUIT OF SAYING "YES, LORD"

I knew early on that I would not leave Nyack the same man as when I arrived. But I had no idea how radically God would deal with me throughout my three years at the school.

The most significant event in my gradual transformation happened early in my senior year. I always looked forward to Friday night, because that was the evening Wanda and I finally got to go out on our weekly date. It didn't matter that the date was always to the school missionary meeting and that it had to be with at least two other couples. (At least we were permitted to have dinner together prior to the service.) It was the highlight of my week. Wanda was always beautiful. I called her "my dove." I was thankful I could sit next to her for a few hours.

The hardest part about Friday nights was the invitation that climaxed each missionary service. After an inspirational message, the visiting missionary would always challenge us to ask God if it was His will for us to answer the call to take the gospel abroad "to the farthest reaches of the earth." This part of the service always made me feel queasy. I didn't like it, because in my heart I knew that Howard Jones didn't want to go abroad; he wanted to be a pastor right here in the States.

Wanda had responded to the invitation early on during our freshmen year. In fact, both she and her sister, Ruth, went forward that Friday. But I wouldn't go. My feet were planted. Wanda often told me, "You should do it so our lives will be completely yielded." But I wasn't budging.

I managed to withstand the pressure to go forward for two full school years. In the meantime, I did things that expressed my commitment to "support the work of missionaries." I joined the Africa Prayer Band, a small club of students who prayed regularly for Africa and African missions. But I saw no need to avail myself to that particular work. Besides, what sending agency would accept a Negro missionary anyway? Wanda told me that was beside the point, that our obligation was to be available to God and that He would take care of the rest. Nevertheless, I remained noncommittal.

Finally, on a fateful Friday in 1943, a missionary from some South American nation that I cannot recall anymore delivered a stirring sermon. He spoke of dying to oneself for the sake of the gospel, of recklessly abandoning oneself to the work of God's kingdom.

In truth, I'd heard a lot of those themes before—like every Friday night. But this time, for whatever reason, the Holy Spirit would not leave me alone. That missionary's words lodged in my heart and I knew my perfect Friday night record of avoidance was over. Before I could wrest control of my emotions, tears were running down my cheeks. I stood to my feet and walked forward without a second thought. "Here I am, Lord," I said. "Whatever You want is what I want. I'll go wherever You want me to go."

And just like that, Howard Jones was once again transformed. Just three years before, I had been saved from sin, emptiness, and death. Now, my "salvation" was from something that for the longest while seemed even more enslaving—my plans for ministry. Finally, I was liberated from my own ideas of how I should serve God and was made free to answer His call to wherever and whatever.

AN INVITATION TO HARLEM

Throughout my final year at Nyack, I preached each weekend in New York, usually at a small Bible class for teenagers in Harlem. The women who started the class, Lydia Borchert and Doris Woolward, hoped to eventually to turn the class into a church plant. One day they approached me with a request: Would I become the founding pastor of the church after I graduated? Lydia, who worked as a secretary of the Nyack headquarters of The Christian and Missionary Alliance denomination, was white, while Doris, a seamstress in a downtown factory, was black. Several years before, they had started holding Bible classes in homes of a few young people who lived in a neighborhood that the Lord had placed upon their hearts. The vision to start a church had sprouted, and now the group was established enough to need a pastor.

Wanda and I agreed to pray and give serious consideration to the opportunity. I remained wide open to go wherever God directed. Somewhere in the deepest parts of my heart, I sensed that our ultimate destination would be somewhere abroad. However, Wanda and I realized that there did not seem to be any wide-open doors for us to travel to a foreign mission field, but that maybe God was calling us to a "mission field" right here in the States, in the heart of the inner city.

We continued to pray, until finally the answer seemed clear. Yes, we would take the job.

Goodbye, Nyack. Next stop: Harlem.

But first, we had some business to attend to back home in Oberlin.

PART THREE

Harlem, Africa, and Beyond

EIGHT

"*Reverend* Jones"

JUST GETTING STARTED

On June 24, 1944, four weeks after our graduation from the Nyack Missionary Training Institute, Wanda and I were finally married. The ceremony, held at Fairchild Chapel on the Oberlin College campus, was wonderful. Wanda was breathtakingly gorgeous in her dazzling white dress. As she walked down the aisle toward me, I offered a quiet prayer of thanks to God.

I looked at Wanda that special day and recalled all the incredible ways the Lord had worked to bring us together—and to ground our relationship in His purposes. All the tears, all the fears and uncertainties, all the long periods of waiting and praying had been God's way of preparing us for this day and all the exciting days to come. I had no idea what adventures would follow once we officially began our ministry together in Harlem, but I was joyously looking forward to the journey.

The next morning, Wanda and I began a practice that

would become our daily habit for the next five decades. I opened my Bible to Jeremiah 33:3 and read aloud: "Call unto me, and I will answer thee, and shew thee great and mighty things, which thou knowest not" (KJV). That passage would become our life verse. Next, we both prayed for our day—and our new life together. I'm so happy we set the tone for our marriage that day. From then on, we would begin each day in eager anticipation of God's blessings, lessons, and surprises. There would be many.

Our brief honeymoon began with a boat trip across Lake Erie to Ann Arbor, Michigan, where we relaxed for the weekend in a nice hotel. While we were in Ann Arbor, a friend named John Wesley Wright heard we were in town and invited me to preach at his church on Sunday morning. Young preachers, of course, rarely turn down speaking opportunities, so Wanda and I spent our first Sunday as husband and wife at the First African Methodist Episcopal Church in Ann Arbor.

Wright was an outstanding preacher who led a huge congregation accustomed to blockbuster sermons each week. So the pressure was on for me to deliver a message that would hold the people's attention and not bring shame and disgrace to my new bride or myself.

That Sunday morning, Wanda and I were dressed in our finest attire. This, after all, was our introduction to the world as a ministry couple. I was proud of my beautiful wife. With her by my side, I felt as though I could conquer any challenge the Lord brought our way.

Reverend Wright introduced me to his congregation. I sat in a pew behind the pulpit. From my vantage point up front, I could see the bright faces of all the churchgoers. I was par-

ticularly drawn to the serious but friendly demeanor of all
the deacons and church trustees seated in the front pews;
each man was immaculately dressed in his black suit, white
shirt and tie.

"I met this young man and his new wife at Mount Zion
Baptist Church in Oberlin, Ohio, a long time ago," Reverend
Wright announced. "And when I heard he was coming here, I
wanted him to preach in our church. So please welcome Reverend Howard Jones." The congregation applauded as I settled into the pulpit. (Of course, the title "Reverend" was not
technically correct just yet. I would soon receive a license
through the C&MA to pastor the church in Harlem; however, I would not be officially ordained as a Christian minister until September 1946. But I liked the sound of that title
and was happy to wear it.)

As I opened my Bible and began preaching, I noticed a gigantic pitcher of water on the right side of the pulpit
counter. After a few minutes of gabbing, I began to loosen
up and found a nice preaching rhythm. The Holy Spirit was
moving, the congregation was shouting, and man, I was feeling good in the Lord!

"Preach!" the church yelled, urging me on. And suddenly,
caught up in the moment, I swung my right hand through the
air to emphasize some dramatic point and accidentally connected with the big pitcher of water. As the pitcher went
sailing off the pulpit toward the congregation, its contents
went raining into the first row. I could see the moment tran-
spiring as if it were in slow motion. That morning, all the
deacons and trustees in their fine black suits were baptized a
second time.

I apologized profusely, but those deacons weren't the only

ones who felt all wet. Instead of finishing my sermon, I really wanted to go find a seat behind a woman with a big hat and hide. After a stunned silence, the congregation exploded in laughter. I saw Wanda covering her face and couldn't determine whether she was laughing or cringing. Either way, it was not my best moment. It was a tough spot for a young preacher.

Thankfully, Reverend Wright stood up and put his arm around me. "It's all right, brother," he told me. Then he addressed the church, "I just want to tell you that this young man is on his honeymoon this week, so you've got to pardon his excess energy." The congregation laughed again, and I was able to continue my message with at least a bit of dignity restored. However, to this day I'm always leery of objects sitting on the pulpit while I'm preaching.

NEW YORK STATE OF MIND

With the honeymoon over, Wanda and I hopped on a train and headed back to New York—and to our new life as the first couple of a new church. Since our church in Harlem could pay me only three dollars a week as starting salary, our first home was a cozy little room in Miss Woolward's fourth-floor apartment in the Bronx where we weren't required to pay rent or buy food.

Miss Woolward was a single woman from St. Kitts in the Caribbean who worked long hours as a seamstress, so she assured us it would be a good living arrangement for us. I remember the day we moved in: Wanda and I didn't have much, but it was a challenge lugging our stuff—my large wooden desk and the trunk that contained everything else we possessed (wedding gifts, a little Sears radio, and my theology books)—up those four narrow flights of stairs.

Even more challenging was adjusting to the new city noises that echoed into our little room; the elevated subway train, which ran right outside our front window, was the primary culprit. This was especially frustrating in the early morning hours, when I would do my sermon and Sunday school preparation for the week. It took time to grow accustomed to the racket, but soon Wanda and I were as thick-skinned and resilient as any longtime city dweller.

With our housing covered, I focused my energies on getting the church on its feet. Our first meeting place was in Harlem on 115th Street and Park Avenue. We met in the upstairs apartment over the local Spanish-speaking C&MA church. In addition to Miss Woolward and Mrs. Borchart (the founders), there were about sixteen others. We fixed up the facilities and called it Bethany Chapel. Slowly word spread about the new Christian and Missionary Alliance congregation, and each week it seemed a new person joined our little church-plant experiment.

Many Sunday evenings I'd be preaching to the group and some of the teenagers from the neighborhood would climb the steps and park themselves in the hallway outside our premises to shoot craps. As I preached, I could hear them out there chitchatting: "Yeah," they'd say, "here's a seven coming up." And then the dice would hit the church door. After a while of listening to this, I'd say to the folks, "Hold on a minute," then I'd go outside, chase those boys down the steps and away from our door, and then try to resume my message without appearing too flustered.

SOLDIERS FOR CHRIST

Soon, I felt God opening my eyes to an incredible mission opportunity that was knocking at our door. Every day I saw young people who needed hope in a hopeless world. And because their parents weren't offering it, they desperately needed the church. I decided to make our little church a refuge for these youths who needed to know someone cared about them. We prayed regularly for ways to reach young people.

As I built relationships with other black pastors and youth leaders across the New York area, God inspired an idea in me that gradually took on a life of its own. I would start an inter-denominational, interracial youth ministry that could attract hundreds of young people with music, activities, and the Good News of Jesus Christ.

God eventually led me to two other black ministers, Ralph Greenridge and Lester Holden, and together we start-ed a series of Saturday night youth rallies called Soldiers for Christ. I was beginning to develop a reputation as an up-and-coming minister in New York, so the rallies attracted a lot of interest.

In those days at the close of World War II, it wasn't unusual to see people on the street corners preaching for one cause or another. We adopted this method to get the word out about Soldiers for Christ. I would take a handful of young people from our church and we would hit the streets. The kids would sing and share their testimonies to draw a crowd, and then I would deliver brief gospel messages that would conclude with an invitation to come out to the various churches where we would hold the Soldiers for Christ rallies.

In time we were drawing hundreds of youths to churches throughout Harlem, Manhattan, Brooklyn, and the Bronx. We rejoiced as each week droves of young people of different races packed the sanctuaries, and by the end of the evenings, many flocked forward to accept Christ into their hearts. It was a resounding confirmation of our ministry in New York.

NINE

Bigger Things
RADIO, BIBLES, AND BABIES

The Lord blessed the work of Bethany Chapel. As our numbers swelled, we began to outgrow our meeting place. Fortunately, our resources were growing as well. Soon we raised enough money to start a legitimate building fund. The question was: What could we afford?

For weeks I had noticed a Jewish synagogue up in the Bronx. It was a nice little congregation of faithful people, but attendance had been dwindling. One day I visited the synagogue and spoke to the presiding rabbi. As it turned out, he couldn't afford to keep the synagogue open anymore and wanted to sell the building. He wanted eight thousand dollars for the property. Our church had only two thousand. So we talked to officials at the C&MA district offices, and they voted to give us the balance of the building's cost. It was an answer to prayer.

Though The Christian and Missionary Alliance Church was a predominantly white denomination, it did work to build bridges across races and cultures for the gospel—not only in foreign lands but also here in the United States. This set the C&MA apart from many white denominations in those days which seemed to turn a blind eye to the plight of Negroes, Hispanics, and other ethnic communities that populated the nation's cities.

A month or so later, after the synagogue had moved out, our congregation—which now numbered about one hundred members—moved in. And Bethany Chapel became Bethany Alliance Church.

Along with the church facilities came a second-floor apartment. Wanda and I finally would be able to move out of our cramped quarters at Miss Woolward's apartment and have a place of our own. This was ideal timing, because the Jones family was growing as well. Our beautiful daughter Cheryl was born August 10, 1945. Two years later, on June 1, her precious sister Gail arrived. And two years after that, on July 4, our lovely Phyllis entered the world. In each instance, my mother traveled from Oberlin to help out until Wanda regained her full strength. Our lives were full, but they were also crowded, so it was wonderful to see the Lord provide a larger living space for our rapidly expanding clan.

We settled into our new church facilities, grateful to God for a place to assemble. Because we had come from a smaller, less user-friendly location, we never complained about the little quirks that came with our building. For instance, in the winter months the hot water pipes banged as though some gremlin were taking a large monkey wrench to them—and they always grew louder right around prayer time. Then there was the air conditioning in the summer—or lack thereof. During the hot and humid months, we usually held our services outdoors. Our joyful singing caused many of our neighbors to lean out their windows to hear us. In fact, several of them would eventually join the church, making it even more difficult for us to complain. It was awesome to watch how God was working in our midst.

ROOM AT THE CAMP

As the Lord blessed our work at Bethany Church, we continued to explore new ways to reach all races and ages for Christ. As often was the case, one of those "new ways" found us.

In the late 1940s and 1950s, Christian summer camps were becoming popular, but only whites were usually encouraged to use such facilities. One of our friends had taken his family to an eastern camp, looking forward to a week of teaching by a renowned Bible teacher. But before dinner on the first day, the camp director knocked on their cabin door, handed back their entire fee and politely asserted that they might be more comfortable worshiping with their "own kind." Not wanting to cause problems, our friends had quietly left the grounds. But their hearts and spirits were broken. This man clearly saw the need for a Christian camp program available to black families. As he discussed his burden with me and other leaders, the vision for a camp was formed.

In God's providence, a Christian woman who owned a tract of farmland two hours away in Bethlehem, Connecticut, wanted to give her property to some group who could use it for God's glory. It was fifty acres of beautiful land spread out on a scenic lakefront. It was the perfect site. We named it "Bethlehem Camp" and launched a Christian camp open to all races. Over the years, we rejoiced to see families and youth groups descend on the place for picnics, camping, and a whole lot of happy worship.

ON THE AIR

One of the most significant developments in our New York ministry began after our first big Soldiers for Christ rally. I had invited Jack Wyrtzen, director of the Word of Life Ministries, to be our inaugural speaker, and he was a big hit. He helped us pack the church with close to a thousand people. No doubt, it was Jack's reputation as a radio minister that helped attract attention to our rally.

Jack Wyrtzen's ministry had started with a small radio program and expanded into a huge evangelistic outreach. As I chatted with him, it occurred to me that God could use radio to take our message to a larger audience. (My friendship with Jack would prove even more providential later in my ministry, but more on that in another chapter.)

I cut a deal with a local station to do a fifteen-minute broadcast of the weekly Soldiers for Christ rally from a different host church each week. We saw the Lord bless this effort, and later decided to move the program to a more powerful station. We were able to get airtime on Sunday nights on WINS, the mighty 50,000-watt New York station. As a result, we began broadcasting the program exclusively from Bethany Church. I brought the Bethany choir in to do a song each week, and my friend Warren Shelton did the closing announcements. It became a special little broadcast.

The radio ministry cost us $113 a week, which was a hefty sum in those days. But the Lord always provided. And we began to see many fruits. People from around the New York area called us and wrote letters telling us how blessed they were by the program. We learned many people had made commitments to Christ as a result of our music and teaching. Some letters came from as far away as Canada.

Radio was a peculiar thing, though, because when listeners hear you on the air, they really don't know who you are—that is, they don't know what you look like. So we'd have white people come to our church on Sunday night for the live broadcast (we opened the invitation at the end of each program), but as soon as they'd walk in and see it was predominantly black, they'd walk out.

One woman, whom I'll call "Mrs. Johnson," had been sending the ministry $100 every other week. And since our weekly expenses were $113, that was quite a significant gift. We were very grateful. She even called us and told us how much she appreciated the program. "We love your preaching," the woman said. "Oh, my, you give the Word. We've adopted you as our radio pastor."

So one week Mrs. Johnson wrote me a letter and sent more money, and then she called me. She said, "We'd like to know. Would you come out to our house in Long Island? We want to meet you face-to-face."

Long Island was quite a distance, but it was difficult to turn down an offer from such a loyal and gracious supporter. So my daughter Cheryl and I made the trek to Mrs. Johnson's home. Cheryl was four at the time, and I often took her places with me when I could to take some of the pressure off of Wanda, who still had two younger ones to look after. Wanda did Cheryl's hair and put her in a cute little dress. She looked so pretty.

So on a pleasant Sunday afternoon, we hopped in the car and made the long journey south. This was the early 1950s, and there weren't many black folk in Long Island in those days, so I knew it was going to be an interesting trip.

We arrived in Long Island about an hour later and found the house. It was an immaculate little mansion, with a neatly manicured lawn and a circular driveway. We parked, walked up to the large wooden door, and knocked. A matronly-looking white woman in her mid-to-late-forties opened the door.

"Mrs. Johnson?" I said.

"Yes."

"I'm Howard Jones."

"You mean *Pastor* Howard Jones?" she said with an incredulous stare.

"Yes," I replied. I could see in her face that she was disappointed.

After a pause that was a few seconds too long, she said, "Oh, please come in."

Cheryl and I walked into her elegant home. I had been in the homes of rich people before, but in this one I got the distinct vibe that I didn't belong. As we moved into the living room to sit, a door opened and a teenage girl popped out, took one look at me, and ran back through the door.

"That's one of my daughters," Mrs. Johnson said uncomfortably. "I might as well tell you right now, Pastor Jones. We didn't know that you were black. And our daughter is afraid of black people."

"That's all right," I said, feeling equally uneasy. I wanted to take Cheryl's hand and make a quick exit, but I sensed God telling me to weather it out. So Cheryl and I sat there across from our wealthy hostess in one of those scenes that neither Mrs. Johnson nor I would have participated in had we known better.

The door opened again and another teenage daughter came in. She seemed far less timid, and actually put Cheryl and me at ease with her warm smile.

"What a beautiful little girl!" the daughter said, looking at Cheryl. "Would you like some cake and milk?"

Cheryl's eyes widened. "Is it all right, Daddy?"

"Yes, honey," I said. So the daughter took Cheryl to the kitchen and closed the door.

There was another chunk of awkward silence, until finally Mrs. Johnson nervously spoke again. "So you're Pastor Howard Jones?"

"Yes, ma'am."

"We've listened to you now for a few years, and I've given you a considerable amount of money."

"I know, and I'm very grateful. It has been a great blessing to our ministry," I said.

"We didn't know that you were a Negro," she said matter-of-factly.

"Should it be of any major concern whether I'm black or white?" I asked as politely as I could manage.

"No, no," she said quickly.

"Color shouldn't mean anything," I continued. "You told me you were blessed by our broadcasts, and that you accepted me as your radio pastor."

"You're right," she said. But I could tell that my skin was a hurdle she wasn't ready to scale.

We talked several minutes more about the ministry, but tiptoed carefully around the subject of race. Finally, the woman's daughter brought Cheryl back. And it wasn't a moment too soon. "Mrs. Johnson," I said, "I've got to conduct a broadcast tonight, so we need to be going."

She smiled and thanked us for coming, but after we drove out of her driveway and back to the Bronx, we never heard from Mrs. Johnson again.

Soon, it became clear that my color presented a major obstacle when it came to attracting supporters for the radio program. Indeed, many times after we'd send ministry materials to someone who had written us to give us a nice donation, we ended up never hearing from those people again. It got so bad that I told Wanda that I wasn't sending out any more literature with our pictures on it. It was too costly.

PASSING THE BOOK

Between my pastorate at Bethany Church, Soldiers for Christ, Bethlehem Camp, and our radio broadcast, my ministry life was sufficiently packed. I quickly became adept at juggling a full and diverse schedule of activities.

One thing I had to work hard to do from the beginning was to build in time for my family. They were with me for mostly all of our church events—Sunday mornings and evenings, Wednesday evenings, and other special times. But I had to be intentional about creating family devotional time. With three energetic young girls of varying ages, it was not easy. But I'm glad I made the commitment to do it early in the life of our family, for it became a stubborn habit that I know continues to this day in the lives of my children's families.

By necessity, I became rather discriminating about the number of new activities I would take on, but from time to time an opportunity would arise that had God's imprint all over it. One such opportunity was my work with the New York Bible Society.

Dr. David Fant, pastor of The Gospel Tabernacle in Times Square, asked me if I'd be willing to head a Harlem branch of the New York Bible Society. Dr. Fant was on the board of the Society, which distributed Bibles to churches and other institutions in the community. The Harlem branch would supply Bibles to the five inner-city boroughs of New York: the Bronx, Brooklyn, Harlem, Manhattan, and Queens. The Bibles would go to hospitals, jails, and needy churches. My job would be to work with African-American communities. After some prayer, I agreed to take on the challenge. It didn't hurt that the position paid a small salary (since my church salary was still meager). The job also allowed for the hiring of a secretary and another part-time assistant.

Our offices were located in Harlem, next door to the famous Apollo Theater. I recruited V. S. Simpson, a young local minister, to help me with the ministry, along with a young woman, Aleta Hamlin, from Oberlin whom I hired as our secretary.

Our big event was the annual Universal Bible Sunday, a huge worship service that would bring together all the participating churches from our five boroughs. It was a big celebration full of music and pageantry. Those Bible Sundays were held at a different church each year.

The biggest Bible Sunday during my three-year tenure took place at the historic Abyssinian Baptist Church, which was led by the legendary preacher and congressman Adam Clayton Powell Jr. Though Powell had a reputation for being rather worldly and extremely political, I asked him if he would be our principal speaker for the event. To my great delight, he agreed. Before he spoke, the great Abyssinian Choir brought the crowd to its feet with a rousing rendition of the hymn "Walking in the Light." Powell's subject that Sunday was "A Living Book for a Dying World." Despite Powell's liberal bent theologically, this was a profoundly biblical message about the importance of God's Word, and the audience loved it.

Though some of my fellow evangelical pastors were surprised at the theological correctness of Powell's sermon, I wasn't. Powell was political, yes. But he knew how to play to his audience.

MOVING ON

During our time in New York City, I had a variety of interesting opportunities for service that went beyond the four walls of Bethany Church. There were youth ministry, radio ministry, a Bible-distribution ministry, and scores of regular speaking engagements at other churches. But after eight years, I sensed my ministry at Bethany Church had reached its peak.

After much prayer, Wanda and I felt God telling us to seek new opportunities. We had seen exciting things. We saw a church grow from a handful of people to well over one hundred committed members. We saw slews of people, young and old, come to Christ through Bethany's ministry and the outreach of Soldiers for Christ. In fact, I am still close to several of those young people to this day. One who comes to mind is Dr. Mildred Clarke, one of the most outstanding gynecological surgeons in New York. At the tender age of thirteen, she was saved at one of our youth meetings. The lives of

Mildred and many others like her gave us confidence that God was in charge of the work we had started in New York, and that He would see it through to completion.

During my eight years in New York, I had often been asked to consider leading a church in Cleveland, Ohio. Earlier, when I sought the Lord's direction on the subject, He seemed to say it wasn't the right time. But in 1952 when the call came again, both Wanda and I knew it was time to move on.

We said tearful good-byes to our dear friends and ministry associates in New York, but we gave thanks for the many souls who were saved and the wonderful work that God saw fit to establish through our efforts.

Throughout my ministry, I've discovered that everything we do now ultimately prepares us for some greater work in the future. This was especially true of our time in New York. All we experienced, all we learned, we soon would put to use in ways we could never have imagined.

TEN

"Welcome to Africa"

FROM CLEVELAND TO THE WORLD

I n early 1952, after eight busy and productive years of ministry in New York, I returned to my home turf of Ohio, where I became pastor of Smoot Memorial Alliance Church of Cleveland. Wanda and I packed our three daughters and ourselves into our secondhand Dodge sedan for the long trip, and my brother, Clarence, traveled from Oberlin with a big truck to help us transport all the stuff we'd collected over the last decade.

It felt great to be returning home. We would miss all the precious relationships and accomplishments made in New York, but there was an exhilarating sense of anticipation of new things. In a way I could relate with the great joy the Prodigal Son must have felt when he walked into his hometown after being on the run for so long—with one big difference. Obviously, my journey away had not been one of carnal living and waste, but of fruitful and God-directed ministry. Still, what a feeling to come home a different person.

I needed New York. Our time there matured my perspective on life and my faith in God. Bethany Church had been a challenging assignment in all ways, but especially financially—especially in the early days when I was making just three dollars a week. Although we initially lived in Miss Woolward's apartment rent-free, there was one day we got down to just a handful of pennies, and I was too proud to write home and ask my dad for money. By that time, Dad had gotten over his displeasure with my career choice. Over the years, he had seen my commitment in preparing for the ministry. And though he never said it aloud, I believe he respected my decision to stand my ground and attend Nyack despite his protestations. In fact, he eventually began sending money to support me at Nyack. My dad was a proud man—but he was also a man who was able to acknowledge his wrongheadedness and change his mind. Most importantly, God had been working in his life to soften his heart and bring him around. Dad gladly would have sent us the money, but I couldn't bring myself to ask.

So Wanda and I went to our bedroom and got down on our knees. And I said, "Oh, Lord, we've just got these pennies. That's all." And suddenly Wanda broke out in laughter. And I shot her a look of mild rebuke. "I'm praying, girl. Why would you break out in laughter? That's sacrilegious."

But Wanda, ever the cool one, said, "Wait a minute, Howard. Isn't the Lord *good?* We have one daughter. She's healthy; we're healthy. We've got a place to stay. We shouldn't be complaining." And then I broke out and started laughing. I said, "That's right."

It was soon after this episode that I started getting invitations to speak at other churches and events, and a little later I was tapped to work with New York Bible Society. With those opportunities came a much-needed infusion of extra income. Times like those revealed God's faithfulness to us in new and marvelous ways. But we would not have experienced those grand, revealing moments of God's grace had we not been forced to dwell in the valleys for a while.

New York prepared me—and my faith—for the numerous other valleys that lurked ahead of us.

SETTLING IN

Smoot Memorial was a church with a rich and historic music ministry. During the 1930s and 1940s it had been the home base of the famed Cleveland Colored Quintet, a group of Spirit-filled men who traveled all over the United States and Europe to share their love for the Lord through music and testimony. On our first Sunday there, we were delighted to hear the splendid voices of the church choir. There are few things that can make an African-American pastor prouder than a joyous and robust choir. I knew at once that I would have at my disposal a powerful tool for ministry.

Smoot was also a pioneering church in the field of black missions. Indeed, from 1913 to 1938, the congregation sent out a cluster of intrepid African-American missionaries to Sierra Leone, West Africa—women and men like Ms. Anita Bolden Fitts, Ms. Carrie Merriwhether, Reverend and Mrs. Eugene Thornley, Reverend and Mrs. Montrose Waite, and Reverend and Mrs. Raymond Wilson. And this gutsy heart for missions, I would discover, was still alive and well within the congregation.

Our new church had a membership of about 200 people

and a healthy turnout of just over 150 every Sunday. I immediately started up a radio ministry. Though Bethany had been
a smaller congregation, my work with Soldiers for Christ and
the New York Bible Society had prepared me for leading a
larger body. And that was good, because there was much to
do at Smoot. There seemed to be programs and classes for
every age and need. Still, it was clear that the foundation of
all ministry at the church was Bible teaching and evangelism
driven by the mandate of the Great Commission to go into
all the world and preach the gospel to every man, woman,
and child. Since this was the impetus for all of my preaching,
I quickly fit in, picking up where I had left off in New York.

At home things were also eventful. Shortly after we settled
in to our new home in Woodmere Village, a Cleveland
suburb, Wanda announced she was pregnant again. So, we ex-
citedly prepared for the arrival of yet another member of our
clan. And with Oberlin just a stone's throw away, this time
our extended family was more intimately involved in the
long, joyful journey to the baby's birth.

Meanwhile, Wanda honed her musical skills by gathering
Cheryl, Gail, and Phyllis around the family room piano and
teaching them to sing in harmony. Wanda and I had sung duets
together at Bethany Church, and we continued to use our
musical gifts at Smoot. But after hearing the girls sing together
one day, Wanda sensed a call to help the girls develop their
voices and ears. It would prove to be an important decision.

One Saturday morning, when Wanda was a few weeks
from her estimated delivery date, she was a little slow getting
out of bed. "I'm feeling a little tired this morning," she explained. But she insisted nothing was wrong and all she
needed was rest. Still, I decided to take her to the hospital,

where the doctors admitted her for observation. I left her there overnight, assuming everything would be all right.

Bad assumption. Just as I was about to begin the worship service the next morning, I heard the phone ring in my office.

"Reverend Jones, this is Doctor Kline," the voice on the other end announced. My heart sank. Was Wanda okay? "I just want to let you know that you have an eight-pound son," Dr. Kline continued. "He was born a half-hour ago. Mother and child are doing fine."

My jaw dropped. I was rendered as speechless as I'd ever been as a preacher on a Sunday morning. "Are you sure?" I finally managed to say. "Are you sure it's a *boy?*"

"Oh, yes," Dr. Kline said with a laugh. "No doubt about it."

I lifted my eyes toward the ceiling and breathlessly gave thanks to God. I cut the service short that morning. But before I excused myself, the congregation and I took a few moments to raise praises to the Lord and rejoice that my son—Howard David Jones—had arrived safely, even if a little ahead of schedule.

The Smoot congregation lovingly embraced all our children, but the church especially took to David—our first child to be born in Cleveland. Wanda and I soon discovered the amazing—and sometimes exasperating—differences between raising little girls and a little boy. We didn't have a church nursery in those days; the babies spent Sundays on their mothers' laps, learning to sit still as toddlers. At least that's how it was supposed to work. David had a mind of his own, and he soon proved he could be very naughty. One Sunday, when David was about three, a parishioner with a

unique voice (some might call it grating) read the Creation
story before the congregation. David listened for several
minutes and then shouted, "Shut up, man!"

Wanda quickly hushed our son, and from my seat on the
platform, I winced. Both Wanda and I wanted to disappear.
But the words had been spoken. The congregation, however,
loved it—the sanctuary was filled with the howl of their
laughter. But that did nothing to abate Wanda's and my em-
barrassment.

Still, despite the occasional face-reddening incidents, both
family life and church life were good. Though different from
the frantic pace of our New York ministry, our time in Cleveland was no less exciting. In fact, with four rapidly sprouting
kids plus a bustling church full of evangelism-minded saints,
we had our work cut out for us.

THE INVITATION

As a preacher, I enjoyed reading periodicals—to keep
abreast of what was happening in the world but also to find
compelling stories and anecdotes I could adapt for sermon
illustrations. *Reader's Digest, Time,* and several religious magazines were on my must-read list. One day as I was catching
up on my reading of *Christian Life* magazine, I ran across a
small advertisement from ELWA, a new 10,000-watt Christian radio station of the Sudan Interior Mission (SIM) in
Monrovia, Liberia. The station was looking for audio tapes
of Negro spirituals produced by black church choirs. According to the ad, the Africans loved Negro spirituals. I realized this could be a ministry opportunity for the Smoot
Memorial choir. So in the week that followed, I rallied the

members of our choir (including Wanda), and we recorded well-known spirituals—tunes such as "Every Time I Feel the Spirit," "Deep River," and "Swing Low, Sweet Chariot." We prayed over the project like any other ministry effort and shipped it off to ELWA (which stood for "Eternal Love Winning Africa").

I was pleasantly surprised when, a few weeks later, the radio station responded enthusiastically about the tape. The letter from ELWA program director Dick Reed read: "We want to put you on prime time with both singing and a short message." They told us we'd be able to reach a good portion of Africa with our program. So, naturally, our church was excited about this new outreach opportunity. We immediately arranged to send more tapes. Dick Reed instructed me to introduce myself in a similar fashion each time. He suggested I say, "This is Howard Jones, a Negro pastor from Cleveland, Ohio, in the United States." When the Africans heard that, they'd know I was black.

We began sending tapes of our music and preaching on a regular basis. By this time, Wanda's little experiment with our young daughters had turned into a full-blown ministry. Cheryl, Gail, and Phyllis—a.k.a. "The Jones Sisters Trio" —sounded extraordinary together. Their angelic harmonies had stirred listeners at Smoot Memorial and many other local churches. So I decided to include a few of their songs on our tapes to Africa, and they were enthusiastically received.

The short sermons I would include on the recordings were simple salvation messages that transcended culture: "It doesn't matter who you are," I would say. "Christ died for all. He died for black people; He died for white people; He died for male and female, young and old.

"The tremendous African audience that's listening to me today, I want you to know this is a message to Africa as well as a message to United States and other nations around the world: You've got to repent of your sins. What do I mean by *repent*? I mean you may be walking in one direction, but the Lord gets a hold of you and turns you around. So to repent means to change your mind about sin, your attitude, and then it means to reverse your position. Maybe you've been walking in one area of life with sin. You can turn away from it, right now. Turn your back on that old sinful life and embrace a new life in Christ.

"If you're listening to me right now and you are guilty of your sins and going through a hellish marriage and on drugs or dope, wherever you are, right here at this point, I'm going to give you that chance to repent right now. You can give your heart to Christ at this very moment. And then you write to this station and tell us what the Lord did in your life, and we'll send you some helpful literature to get you started in the Christian life."

After just a few weeks of sending our tapes to ELWA, we were inundated with mail from Liberians who had been converted through our program. They said it was the first time they had ever heard the voice of an American black man. And consequently, our program became ELWA'S most popular broadcast.

Soon, our radio program mushroomed to the point where the SIM staff invited me to come to Africa to preach to the people in person. They asked if I would conduct a three-month series of evangelistic meetings in Liberia, Ghana, and Nigeria. If I went, I would be the first black evangelist to hold crusades of such magnitude in West Africa, their letter said. In fact, the whole idea was an experiment to survey the nationals' response to an American black clergyman. Several white missions had agreed to sponsor the tour—if I would agree to go.

I immediately thought back to that fateful Friday evening at Nyack when I had once and for all told God I would go wherever He led me. I had no idea then that the place might be Africa—in fact, we had always been told how unlikely that would be for a Negro missionary. But there I was, just a "Yes" away from not only one of the most significant decisions of my life, but also one that would have widespread importance for evangelical missions in general.

Obviously, I had to pray.

It was not an easy decision, but after many hours of deep prayer and reflection—along with godly counsel from trusted friends and family members—both Wanda and I sensed God's hand in the opportunity to tour Africa. What's more, our church was willing to back us with their prayers and financial support.

Of course, the most difficult part was leaving behind our four precious children for three whole months. At first, I thought Wanda would remain at home with them. But as our prayers became more focused and intense, we saw God opening the door for Wanda to accompany me on the trip.

Providentially, the Lord brought a loving, trustworthy couple in our church who were between housing situations to gladly volunteer to take care of our children while we were away.

So with the strong prayers of many faithful believers across the country and zeal to take God's Word to the farthest

reaches of the earth, Wanda and I embarked on our most am-
bitious journey yet. "Well, sweetheart," I told my wife as we
sat in the plane, "I promised to take you around the world,
and here we go. God just had a different plan for our travels."

TO A LAND FAR, FAR AWAY

In January 1957, we arrived in Liberia to great fanfare.
Being the first black American clergyman to hold major
evangelistic rallies in West Africa turned out to be a cause for
great celebration in the country. When we got off the plane,
awaiting us were our hosts Ray de la Haye, ELWA'S superin-
tendent, and his wife, Sophie, along with ELWA members
Dick and Jane Reed, Bill and Betty Thompson, and others.
And standing next to them was Mrs. Tolbert, the wife of Vice
President William Tolbert of Liberia. If we had any doubts up
until then that this was a special occasion, they were wiped
away at that moment.

As we traveled through Monrovia and smaller villages, the
people went crazy. It was as if we were the Beatles arriving in
America for the first time, except we weren't importing rock
'n roll but the Rock of Ages.

There were large banners and signs strung across the
streets welcoming us to Africa and announcing our crusade.
Liberia's president William V. S. Tubman hosted a special ban-
quet in our honor. The Liberian people beat drums, chanted,
and said, "Praise the Lord, the big bird has brought our
brother and sister from America." Wanda and I looked at each
other, overwhelmed at how much of a joyous spectacle our
presence there inspired.

We quickly understood that a big reason for the people's

excitement was the fact that we were black Americans. Wherever we went, people would squeeze our hands tightly, pull us toward themselves and say, "Where have you been? We've seen the white missionary, but we've never seen a black preacher from America."

Time after time, the question would come again like a stubborn echo: Where were all the *black* American missionaries?

The West African people had heard about the big, vibrant Negro churches in America, yet they only saw *white* missionaries coming to Africa. Why didn't the black churches send doctors, teachers, and ministers? Didn't the black American Christians care about their brothers and sisters in Africa?

Indeed, black American Christians had been conspicuously absent from the missions scene in those days. But the real reason behind their absence was not apathy but ignorance and institutional racism. Few black Christians were encouraged to become part of international mission works.

Blacks actually were among the first American missionaries to live and work in Africa. One of the most prominent among them was the Reverend Lott Carey, who was born a slave near Richmond, Virginia, and was hailed as the first black Baptist missionary to Africa. In the early 1800s, Carey formed an African missionary society and raised funds to sail to West Africa, where he founded missions in Liberia and Sierra Leone.

But by the early twentieth century, when colonial governments controlled large portions of Africa, black Americans were denied visas and blocked from servings as missionaries. Part of the reason was colonial anxiety that black missionaries would incite rebellion and inspire calls for liberation among Africans.

Then there were the other more mundane reasons—many of which we had heard mouthed at Nyack: the children of black missionaries wouldn't be able to mix with the white missionary kids, Africans would "drag" black missionaries to "their level," et cetera. To discourage blacks from applying for mission service, many white sending agencies engineered racist application structures that were similar to the unconstitutional literacy tests many southern U.S. states required blacks to take before they would be allowed to vote. Consequently, prospective black missionaries often didn't meet the stringent academic, marital, or theological requirements that many white mission-sending agencies demanded.

For these and other reasons—such as a failure among many black church leaders to promote the importance of missions to their congregations—there were only scant numbers of black Americans doing work on foreign mission fields. When I had time, I explained this history to my West African friends. But usually my standard response to their inquiries was something like, "Many of us would have liked to come, but the mission agencies held us back." Thankfully, ELWA radio, the Sudan Interior Mission, and other mission organizations defied the conventional thinking among white evangelical groups of that era and worked to extend the privilege of missionary service to black Americans.

TWISTS AND TURNS

Some people who had heard me on the radio doubted I was Howard Jones because I looked too young. In their culture, wisdom and authority was normally associated with bald heads and portly guts, and I had neither.

Many were also surprised by my light complexion. Some even doubted I was black, until they ran their hands through my hair.

Throughout the cities and bush countries, people turned out by the thousands, some walking as far as forty miles to get to the crusade meetings. We learned from friends back home that *Time* magazine had done a short feature on our evangelistic tour. The curiosity of a *Negro* evangelist drawing massive crowds in Africa proved to be too much for even the mainstream press to ignore.

At each stop I was assigned a translator who skillfully relayed my English preaching into the language and dialect of the region. While traveling through Liberia, Wanda and I were introduced to Wilfred and Betty Quimby, a black couple who were full-time American missionaries in the country. They were a fine couple whose ministry was an exception to the "all-white missionary" rule. The Quimbys, however, spent most of their time in the rural "interior" areas of the country, so many of the urban nationals who turned out for our crusade were not familiar with them or other black missionaries who served in the interior.

I discovered that Wilfred had a wonderful solo voice, so I asked him if he would join me for the rest of our tour, and he agreed. His singing set the perfect tone of praise and worship before I took to the podium to declare the gospel.

One of the unusual surprises of addressing the large crowds was the manner in which they responded to a speaker or singer. I had to get used to the soft clicking noise that the crowds would make with their mouths to express their joy and approval. Often when I would have expected to hear applause, the outdoor air was filled with their delightful clicking.

I was especially pleased that Wanda also had the opportunity to share special messages with the female members of the crowds. At first, she was hesitant to address such large crowds. But after much prayer, and some gentle nudging from her husband, she rose to the challenge and presented heartfelt talks that I believe truly ministered to the women.

In Ghana our tour schedule was packed. Most of the crusades were held during the day, since there was limited electricity for lights. So sometimes I was asked to share a brief message four or five times in an afternoon. Though my body soon began to acknowledge the effects of such a demanding schedule, God always supplied the extra strength and grace needed to move on to our next appointment.

Whether it was Liberia, Ghana, or Nigeria, the response was the same. The people were hungry for the Word of God, and they responded in gigantic droves to my invitation to receive Christ.

Our travels had gone off without a hitch for the most part, until several weeks into the tour. One morning we had breakfast with one of the respected Ghanaian politicians. He was a Christian, and we were guests at his home, a beautiful house constructed of stone. About midday, Wanda complained that she wasn't feeling well and began to have a vomiting spell. She became so weak that she had to lie in bed the rest of the day.

I called a doctor. He examined her and concluded that she was suffering from food poisoning. Wanda had consumed some bad fish for breakfast that morning. The doctor suggested we admit her in a local hospital, which we did right away.

For the next two days, she continued to vomit and could barely move from her bed. She wasn't getting any better. So I sent a wire to the SIM hospital in Jos, Nigeria, the Bingham Hospital (a fine medical institution), and I talked to the doctor. I told him I'd feel better if my wife could be at his hospital, and he said they'd send a plane right away.

Soon Wanda and I were off on the two-hour plane trip to the SIM hospital. After getting her admitted, I realized I had a tough decision to make. The crusade tour was at a crucial point in Ghana at this time, and thousands were counting on me to preach in their cities and villages. In her brief moments of lucidity, Wanda encouraged me to carry on with the tour. But I was not convinced. We were in this foreign land, thousands of miles away from home. How could I leave her alone there? "Dear Lord," I prayed, "what should I do?"

At once, I felt God directing me to keep my commitments and trust Him (and the able staff at the hospital) to take care of my beloved Wanda. So I uttered a desperate prayer of protection and healing over my wife and left to resume the busy crusade schedule.

Though I flew back to Jos to see Wanda whenever I could, I was essentially separated from my dear wife for about a month. When Wanda was finally well enough to rejoin the tour, she joined us for the meetings in Nigeria. At first I made sure she took it slow, but soon she was back in ministry mode, speaking to crowds of women and loving every minute of it.

GOING HOME

Our West African tour was one of the most life-changing and profound experiences of our lives, but Wanda and I had missed our children from the moment we'd left three months earlier. We knew it was time to get home to them, even though our hearts were full of love and affection for the people of Liberia, Ghana, and Nigeria.

Our tour officially came to a close in Kano, northern Nigeria, a land where the aroma of peanuts permeates the air. When we prepared to board the Pan Am clipper back to the States, the African people were crying—and so were we.

"Pastor Jones," they said. "Go home and get your children and come back. We need you. We love you."

The prospect of us returning to Africa to stay was not a far-fetched idea. Both Wanda and I had frequently entertained the notion of extending our ministry there. In fact, when we were preparing to leave the ELWA headquarters in Monrovia several weeks earlier, Mrs. de la Haye had taken Wanda down by the ocean to look at lots where we might build a home. The two women actually placed a stake at one particularly scenic lot overlooking the sea and prayed for God's will to be done. "Wanda, I believe God's going to bring you and your family back here," Mrs. de la Haye said.

And in my heart, I knew Mrs. de la Haye was on to something. I felt we were going to come back. When I had left Cleveland three months earlier, I had told the congregation, "When we come back, we're going to build a new church." But when I got to Africa, preaching to thousands of people and seeing the Lord save souls in miraculous ways, I forgot all about building a physical church. I was in a spiritually famished land building *the* church, the Church of Jesus Christ.

When we got back to Cleveland, Wanda and I couldn't hug and kiss our kids long enough. David, who was now five, had grown so much. I could see Cheryl, Gail, and Phyllis blossoming into beautiful young ladies. While we were away, they had continued to develop their music ministry as The Jones Sisters Trio and had performances lined up for months to come.

We were also thrilled to see our church family at Smoot Memorial. As I stood in the pulpit our first Sunday back, the church was packed. Afterward, there was a noticeable buzz among my parishioners. "That was a powerful sermon the pastor gave," I could hear some say. "But do you detect something different about him?"

And, of course, they were right. I *was* different—a different preacher and a different man. I had always possessed an evangelist's heart, but before it had been within the context of my primary role as a local-church pastor. Now that passion had grown, and I knew my calling had changed along with it.

When an unexpected letter arrived from New York a few weeks later, it was further evidence God might have a different plan for my ministry—and for the Jones family.

ELEVEN

The Letter

A MOMENTOUS CALL FROM THE GARDEN

When Jack Wyrtzen's letter came in May 1957, it was the last thing that I was expecting. Jack, you may remember, was the director of Word of Life Ministries in New York. As evangelists and radio broadcasters, Jack and I had a lot in common. We had become good friends while I was in New York, but I hadn't spoken to him for a long time, so I was pleasantly surprised to see his name in the left corner of the envelope.

In his letter Jack explained that he had recently had breakfast with America's most prominent evangelist, Billy Graham. At that time Billy had just begun his massive New York crusade in Madison Square Garden. During his meeting with Jack, Billy lamented the fact that in the opening days of his crusade the crowds had been virtually all white. How could that be in a city as diverse as New York? The minority turnout had been dreadful, and Billy, who had pledged never to conduct another segregated crusade following the 1954

Brown v. Board of Education of Topeka Supreme Court ruling against segregation in public schools, wanted to practice the social justice he had been espousing.

Billy already had integrated his team with Akbar Abdul-Haqq, a gifted preacher from India, but now he wanted to add a black team member to his lineup—which he knew was a riskier proposition.

"Do you know of any Negro evangelists whom we can add to our team?" Billy had asked, knowing Jack was firmly plugged into the New York Christian community. Implicit in his question was the idea that this Negro evangelist had to be someone who could transcend racial boundaries; someone whose theology was sound and whose approach was non-threatening; someone who understood the subtle intricacies, the manner and vernacular of white evangelical culture. In short, someone who was safe.

It didn't take Jack long to submit his recommendation. "Billy, you need to get Howard Jones," he said.

"I think I've read about him in *Time* magazine," Billy said. "Could you help me contact him?"

And that is where I entered the picture.

I was thrilled to receive the letter, because Wanda and I were planning a trip to New York anyway to visit our old church, Bethany Alliance, and share with them stories of our exciting campaign in Africa. I said to Wanda, "While we're there in New York, we should go to Madison Square Garden one night and listen to this man, Billy Graham."

I contacted Billy's office and arranged a meeting with him for the night that we would be at the crusade. I had no clue at the time how significant and far-reaching that meeting would be.

MEETING BILLY

Returning to New York was a moving experience. We were able to catch up with our old friends and colleagues, plus we checked in on how the various ministries we'd left behind were doing. God, of course, was faithful. Bethany Church, Soldiers for Christ, and the Bible Society had continued to grow and prosper after our departure. It was a bittersweet visit. While we were happy to see our friends and the fruits of our work, we also felt a twinge of sadness that we were no longer there. Still, we knew God had moved us on for a reason. And our recent trip to Africa was a vivid indication of that.

Wanda and I were privileged to attend one of the early meetings of the Madison Square Garden crusade. We sat in the arena taking in the marvelous sights and sounds. We enjoyed the inspiring praise songs of the crusade choir led by Billy's music director and emcee, Cliff Barrows, and we were blessed by the wonderful singing by Billy's longtime soloist, George Beverly Shea. To hear Billy's preaching and see the tremendous crowd that came forward after his invitation to receive Jesus Christ as Savior was an unforgettable experience.

When we arrived at the Garden, I had made it known to the crusade officials that I was present, and Grady Wilson, one of Billy's chief team members, came to me and said, "Howard, Billy would like to see you in his office after the conclusion of tonight's meeting."

So Wanda and I were escorted to Billy's temporary New York headquarters, and there I saw him lounging in a chair, relaxing after that evening's understandably exhausting presentation. He jumped up to greet us, and I immediately was taken with how tall and handsome the man was. He walked over and gave me a big bear hug and warmly shook Wanda's hand.

"God bless you, brother," he said in his distinctive North Carolinian drawl. "We've heard about your great meetings in Africa, and I am so happy you could come." He motioned for us to sit down and asked his assistants to bring us some water.

"I want to tell you about the burden that is on my heart," Billy continued, as he returned to his chair. "We are having a fantastic crusade here in New York City. We had planned to go two weeks and are now into the fifth week of meetings. It just looks as if God wants us to go on. As you know, I don't like the fact that our crowds have been all white, and I want to integrate these meetings. But I don't know how to do it." He looked at me enthusiastically. "Would you be willing to come here and work with us for a few weeks to help us with this issue of integration?"

My eyes lit up. I was frankly overwhelmed by such an incredible opportunity. But almost immediately, I thought of my parishioners at Smoot Memorial Church.

"Billy," I said, "I am humbled by this tremendous invitation. But I have been away from my church for three-and-a-half months, and I don't know how they will react if I ask them to give me more time away from the church."

He paused for a long moment, and then it was as if a light bulb went on in his mind. "Would it be all right if I wrote them a letter requesting your presence here?" he finally asked.

"Well, sure," I said.

We spent several minutes praying over the matter, and

then he promised that he'd send the letter to us very soon. He hugged us, and we departed.

THE CHURCH VOTE

As Wanda and I traveled back to Cleveland, we both remarked at how impressed we were with this man's sincerity and love and his passion to reach all people. We recalled the news report about the tense moment a few years earlier when Billy courageously tore down the ropes that separated the races at a Mississippi crusade and declared his intention to never hold segregated meetings again. What a bold and prophetic stand.

In my heart, I was ecstatic about the possibility of helping Billy advance his work in New York. But my heart was torn. What about my people at Smoot Memorial?

When I returned to Smoot's pulpit the next Sunday, I asked that all of our members remain in the sanctuary after the morning service.

"I have some very important business that I want to discuss with you," I told them. Then I read the letter that Billy had addressed to the church. When I was finished, I said, "You can see here that Reverend Graham has asked me to join the team as his first Negro evangelist, to help him break down racial barriers at his New York crusade. It is true that I have been away three-and-a-half months, but I would like to go and work with Reverend Graham. Nevertheless, I have to bring this before the church, the board, and all of you. What is your pleasure?"

I waited anxiously, not knowing how they would respond. Then, after a full thirty seconds, one of the chief men in the church stood up and said, "Well, speaking for myself and, I hope, on behalf of our church, I am just thrilled! I think as a church we ought to be honored that the world's great evangelist, Billy Graham, would invite our pastor to work with him in the New York crusade.

"Now it's true that our pastor has been away for more than three months," the man continued, looking at the congregation, "but I am sure we can get some preachers to fill the pulpit while he is away. I would like to put forth a motion for the church to let Pastor Jones go to New York to do the work that God is calling him to do."

Another member seconded the vote, and everyone agreed. The church voted unanimously to send me back to New York.

TWELVE

New York, New York

BREAKING DOWN BARRIERS
IN THE BIG APPLE

I was sitting on the platform at Madison Square Garden before 18,000 New Yorkers who had come to hear Billy Graham preach. Seated with me on the stage were a dozen other pastors and civic leaders. We were all people of faith—Christians who loved the Lord. However, one thing set me apart from the other men on the platform: I am black.

There's a mixed blessing to being the first African American to realize some key achievement in the United States. It is an honor to overcome a barrier that has long kept blacks on an unequal footing with whites. But, along with the outer triumph, there is an inner ache—an angst—of having to live with the often unfriendly fallout of going where no black man has ever gone before. It's feeling that you're a living experiment, a human lab test. It's the pressure of knowing your every word and action has the potential to make or break the hopes of millions of others who will come after you.

I was acutely aware of this pressure on that summer day in 1957. I had agreed to become the first African-American associate on Billy Graham's team of evangelists, but I had not taken a hard look at the racial ramifications of my decision. I had a call from God to preach the gospel of Jesus Christ. That was my priority. Soon, though, I was forced to look at the matter through the American social prism of black and white.

Back in 1957 we were just three years removed from the landmark *Brown v. Board of Education* case that opened the doors for racial integration in the United States, and we were still a few years away from Martin Luther King Jr.'s rise to national prominence. It was a different world.

Today when African-American actors such as Denzel Washington or Halle Berry win Academy Awards, people of all races celebrate it. Back then, when a figure such as Jackie Robinson broke the race barrier in Major League baseball, he received death threats from fans and dirty looks from members of his own team.

I didn't receive death threats, but I was the recipient of plenty of dirty looks. And when news hit the street that Billy was thinking of bringing me on board, he received an alarming number of disparaging letters: "You should not have a Negro on your team," came the warnings. "You're going to ruin your ministry by adding minorities." "We may have no choice but to end our support."

For better or worse, the church has typically followed the lead of secular society when it comes to our attitudes about race. Today racial reconciliation has become an evangelical buzzword. Organizations such as Promise Keepers proclaim its importance. Christian books, magazines, and musical artists denounce racism and celebrate ethnic diversity in the church. When Billy approached me to join him in New York, it was more or less understood that white Christians worshiped with white Christians, and black Christians worshiped with black Christians. Our evangelical churches seemed to believe that heaven, too, would be "separate but equal." We recited the Apostle's Creed and prayed, "Thy will be done on earth as it is in heaven," but then proceeded to bow at the altar of Jim Crow.

Talk about being countercultural; what Billy did was radical. There's no getting around it. He weathered the barrage of angry letters and criticisms. He resisted the idea of pulling the plug on the whole thing and playing it safe. There was never any hesitation on Billy's part. He remained faithful to his convictions. He had dug the trench, you might say, and he was going through. He knew it was what God was calling him to do.

WHERE THE PEOPLE ARE

In New York, Billy once and for all made it clear that his ministry would not be a slave to the culture's segregationist ways. He was serious about integrating the crowds at his Madison Square Garden crusade, which had registered a disappointing number of blacks during its first several evenings. Soon after my arrival in New York, he looked to me for counsel on boosting minority turnout. "Howard, what can we do to get more blacks to the meetings?" he asked.

I looked at Billy and gave him the hard truth: "If they're not coming to you, you have to go to where they are," I said. "Billy, you need to go to Harlem."

This is a cardinal rule of evangelism and missions: *You have to go where the people are.* Jesus knew this well. When He dined with tax collectors and sinners, He wasn't worried about how it would reflect on His reputation (Matt. 9:9-13). In another instance, while journeying to Galilee he expressed an urgent need to travel through Samaria (John 4:4-43). It wasn't the most politically correct route for a Jew to take in those days, but He made it a point to put Himself where the needs were—where the people were. He was incarnational in every aspect of the term. We can only strengthen our evangelistic efforts by following His example. And Billy did.

Predictably, the prospect of going to Harlem brought Billy even more flack from white church leaders. They warned that it was too dangerous—"Those savages up there will kill you!" Still, Billy made plans to hold a rally in Harlem.

The irony is that some of those whites who were saying "Don't go to Harlem" were members of evangelical churches that were sending white missionaries to Africa. They weren't afraid of ministering to the blacks over there, but the men and women in Harlem were another story.

I worked my New York contacts to spearhead a series of rallies where Billy was able to come before the community's Christian leaders and declare his commitment to them. In Harlem more than 8,000 people turned out to hear the evangelist share his heart. A week later, we organized a similar event in Brooklyn. More than 10,000 blacks and other minorities packed that service.

It was at this Brooklyn rally that Billy remarked publicly for the first time that civil rights legislation—combined with hearts transformed by God's love—would be necessary to eradicate the discrimination and racism that pervaded our nation. This would have been a bold statement for any white conservative preacher in those days; the fact that it was Billy Graham saying it made it even more striking.

God blessed our strategy. The smaller rallies resulted in increased black attendance at the Madison Square Garden crusade. It was estimated at the time that by the conclusion of the New York crusade in August, blacks were making up 20 percent of the nightly crowds.

Famous black actress and singer Ethel Waters attended the crusade meetings one evening and recommitted her life to Christ. When Cliff Barrows discovered that Miss Waters was in the audience, he invited her to sing a solo. Ethel brought the house down with a rousing rendition of "His Eye Is on the Sparrow." After that, she joined the crusade choir and turned down several lucrative performance opportunities to sing at the crusade for the remainder of the meetings.

Billy's friend Martin Luther King Jr., was the other famous African American who appeared onstage at the New York crusade. Billy invited him to come to the Garden one evening to lead a prayer. When the news got out that Dr. King was coming, Billy again got a lot of nasty letters and telephone calls from irate whites. "Why would you invite that communist?" some said. "He's an agitator and an enemy to the peace of America!" Billy's response: "He is my friend, I admire the work he is doing, and I back what he is doing." Again, Billy stood his ground.

Billy also heard from some members of the black community who questioned why he would not allow Dr. King to do more than say a short prayer at the meeting. (Later, in 1963, when Billy decided not to attend King's famous March on Washington, he would again hear it from black leaders who questioned his commitment to racial justice.) I've always responded to Billy's African-American critics by asking them to examine those things Billy *has* done for racial progress. No other white evangelical leader of his prominence put himself on the line for civil rights as much as Billy, even if he did not pass each and every litmus test of the black establishment.

Dr. King did pray at the crusade. That evening after the meeting, Billy threw a party for Dr. King at the New Yorker Hotel in one of the large rooms. He invited a select group of his team members to attend, and he said to me, "Howard, I want you to be there." After an elegant dinner, Billy asked Dr. King a few questions about the race problem in America and invited the civil rights leader to respond at length. Billy asked, "How in the world did you maneuver the Montgomery bus boycott without violence?"

The room got extremely still. Dr. King was the kind of person who would always ponder a question thoroughly before answering, and he did so that night. After a long pause, he finally explained that when Rosa Parks was arrested for not giving up her seat to a white passenger on that fateful December 1956 day in Montgomery, Alabama, he called a meeting of black ministers to discuss a plan of action. The main thing they did at that meeting was pray to God to give them wisdom to address the great injustice that was being inflicted on the black citizens of their city. And so the short answer to the question, said Dr. King, is prayer. They prayed.

It was my privilege that evening to meet Dr. King and shake his hand. He said to me that night, "Brother Jones, I would like to have you come and preach at my church sometime." Of course, I told him I would be honored. Sadly, though, in the course of time our paths would not cross again.

"HOW DID HE GET UP HERE?"

I was pleased to see an increased minority turnout at the New York crusade, but this period was also one of the most agonizing times of my life. With Wanda and the kids still in Cleveland, I was overwhelmed with a sense of loneliness. And it was only compounded by the fact that I was the lone African American on Billy's team. Every evening I felt the piercing stares and heard people muttering under their voices. There were nights when it seemed palpable.

I remember sitting on the crusade platform on various occasions with empty seats next to me because some white crusade participants had decided to sit on the other side of the stage. At other times, I would go down to counsel new believers during the altar calls only to see white counselors move in the other direction.

One night, I heard two white pastors seated behind me murmuring to each other: "How did he get up here?" one of them asked. The other replied, "That's Graham's new associate."

I put on a brave face while in public, but once I was alone the mask came down. There were nights when I went back to my hotel room and wept before God and told Him, "Lord, I can't take this pressure." I felt like telling Billy it was too much. But I knew his heart, and I knew the heart of the team. God gave me the strength to endure.

Eventually, Wanda arranged for some church members to take care of our kids and the Graham Association flew her to New York to be with me. This was a great comfort. Billy's wife, Ruth Bell Graham, was particularly gracious to Wanda when she arrived. "Oh, Wanda. It's so nice to finally meet you," Ruth said as she embraced my wife. "We love Howard, and now we get to spend some time with you as well."

With Wanda by my side again, I felt rejuvenated. Though I still sensed hateful stares from some people, I knew for certain God had brought me to New York for a reason. I looked forward to the remaining nights of the crusade with renewed anticipation.

TORN BETWEEN TWO LOVES

After sixty-eight days, the crusade came to a close. It would go down as the longest crusade in Graham's ministry. When all was said and done, some two million New Yorkers had attended the event, and tens of thousands had made commitments to Jesus Christ.

We rejoiced at God's faithfulness. But the event also had exhausted us. I was happy to return home to Cleveland to see my dear family and my congregation at Smoot Memorial Alliance Church.

A month later, however, I received another call from Billy. This time he wanted me to join his staff full-time. I was thrilled and honored at the request. But I was torn: I loved being a pastor of a local church, but I knew God had given me a passion for evangelism. And when the world's most famous evangelist wants you to work for him, how do you say no?

I told him that I couldn't give him an immediate decision. He told me to take my time, that the invitation was open. For the next year, I poured myself into the pastoral duties at Smoot Memorial, enjoying every moment of it. But at the same time, Wanda and I prayed and fasted regularly for a clear signal from God about our future.

By now, you've probably detected a pattern in my min-istry. I was never the kind of preacher who went out looking for a new gig. But God consistently had something lined up. All I knew was I was called to preach the gospel. I never could have predicted how far and wide that simple call would take me.

Frankly, neither Wanda nor I were prepared for what God had in store for us next.

PART FOUR

Keeping Up with the Joneses

THIRTEEN
Adventures with Billy
BECOMING A FULL-TIME EVANGELIST

In spring 1958 I flew to San Francisco to take part in the Bay Area Billy Graham crusade. Again I worked with Billy's team to help promote minority attendance. Just as in New York, we were effective in networking with black, Hispanic, and other non-white churches to reach those populations and increase their numbers at the event. Bob Harrison, an African-American pastor in San Francisco and a superb piano player, was a key force in getting out the word to the black community. (Bob would later join me on some of my evangelistic tours.)

Immediately following the San Francisco crusade, Billy and I revisited the idea of me joining his team on a full-time basis. After more than a year of persistent prayer on the matter, I was closer to giving him a decision. God had made it clear I was to leave my pastorate in Cleveland and become a full-fledged evangelist. However, there was still the question of *where* I was being called to serve. Billy's invitation offered the tremendous opportunity to travel the world. But ELWA continued to court me, and both Wanda and I sensed that God was calling us back to Liberia.

We were conflicted: *Should we go with Billy, or return to Africa?*

It turned out our worries were for naught. When I told Billy about our dilemma, he suggested we do both. "Howard, we could set up your office and home in Liberia," he said. "Then you could fly out of there from time to time to join me for crusades."

I was thrilled with that arrangement. By His providence, God had answered my family's prayers about our future and given us more than we could have ever dreamed.

Part of the reason for the unique working arrangement was Billy's desire to do a series of crusades across Africa. After much discussion and prayer, he decided to visit eleven countries on the continent, including Liberia, Ghana, and Nigeria—my old stomping grounds. The meetings would launch in January 1960. A few associates and I would do the initial legwork to arrange meetings, network with local churches and missionaries, and train counselors.

When I got back from the San Francisco meeting, Wanda and I stared at each other for the longest time, overwhelmed by the prospect of our future ministry. God was so good to us. Not only would we be able to continue our work with ELWA, but we'd also have the resources and support of the Billy Graham Evangelistic Association (BGEA) at our disposal. What's more, this time our entire family would be able to make the trip.

By the end of the summer, we had made all the necessary

preparations for our next journey: contacting ELWA as to our expected arrival, educating the children on what to expect in their new home, getting shots, and filing all the necessary paperwork. But the hardest part, by far, was making the announcement to our family and friends.

In October I resigned my pastorate at Smoot Memorial Alliance Church. Many tears and extended hugs followed as we said good-bye to those beloved brothers and sisters who had given of their time, their talents, and their pastor to become a "world church"—one whose vision was not limited to its own backyard.

"Thank you for never holding me back from God's call on my ministry—and His call on this church," I told my loyal parishioners, as my eyes moistened. "You have given so much to the cause of the gospel. Keep on taking the good news to all the world, and remember us as we do the same."

Four months later, in February 1959, Wanda and I and our four children climbed aboard the S. S. African Glen cruise ship in the New York harbor and sailed into a bright but uncertain future. We were thankful our entire family would be able to go this time, but we were also keenly aware of the huge life changes that lay ahead for our kids. What happens when the excitement of a big adventure across the world wears off? Would they be able to adjust to a radically different culture?

Yet we knew our children's hearts and minds were securely in God's hands. As the lights of Ellis Island and Lady Liberty faded in the distance, we prayed together that God would guide and protect us during this next chapter of our family's journey.

RETURN ENGAGEMENT

Twelve days later, our ship pulled into the docks of Monrovia. It was like coming home again. Wanda and I had grown so fond of the relationships and spiritual bonds we had established in this faraway land that we couldn't imagine not returning. This time, however, would be different. This time the entire Jones family was present—it would not be a short-term visit but a long-term commitment. This time we were asking to become a lasting part of the community.

Our close friends from ELWA were waiting to meet us at the dock. They helped us load our worldly belongings into a large truck and then escorted us into the city. As we traveled to our newly built home, our children registered fascination and mild amusement at the surreal sight of goats and cars occupying the same streets. At least it was surreal by our American standards. In time many things that seemed unusual to our Western eyes became as common as the rainbow-colored ice-cream trucks that roamed Cleveland's streets each summer.

Soon we arrived at our new house (constructed with funds supplied by the Billy Graham Evangelistic Association). Though it wasn't built on the same property Wanda and Sophie de la Haye staked out on that emotional day two years ago, it was on a gorgeous tract of land overlooking the Atlantic Ocean. The home was an attractive four-bedroom model with a generous sitting room (complete with fireplace) and a patio that faced the ocean. There was plenty of space for our growing family. We toured the place with our ELWA friends Ray and Sophie de la Haye, Dick and Jane Reed, Tom and Cathy Lowe, and Bill and Betty Thompson. We thanked our friends for their kindness and asked them to join us in a prayer of dedication for the house—and for the new adventure ahead.

This period was especially adventurous for our kids, who overcame initial bouts with homesickness to settle into a productive routine in Monrovia. Instead of sending them away to a distant boarding school, we chose to send them to the ELWA Academy. Cheryl and Gail, being the oldest, continued their learning through special correspondence courses. We also gave thanks to God as we saw Wanda's education degree put to good use in the development of our own little students.

Each day began with family devotions, breakfast, and the ritual ingesting of vitamins and various medications that kept our vulnerable American bodies protected from a variety of exotic diseases. The rest of the mornings were spent in study—the children with their school lessons, Wanda in preparation for the new *Women of Faith* radio program she hosted, and I getting my sermon themes and outlines together for my radio show and live crusades. Wanda and I also did a radio show together called *Question Box,* on which we answered questions on spiritual matters from our listeners.

Afternoons were devoted to outreach in the surrounding villages or programming at the studio. Wanda led women's Bible studies during the week in nearby villages and taught a Sunday school class in our living room on Sunday mornings. I made the rounds in the villages, visiting with local church leaders in hopes of adding them to our network.

Between my work with ELWA and my responsibilities with the BGEA, my days never seemed long enough. My favorite moments out on the road were those spent meeting with local people—hearing their stories, sharing Christ's

hope for their hopeless situations. And there were plenty of
seemingly hopeless situations—families ravaged by extra-
marital affairs, alcoholism, and domestic abuse. On the surface, the problems sound like anything you'd find in the
broken lives of an American family. But each situation had
its own unique issues rooted in the African context. It took
long hours of relationship building and cultural acclimatiza-
tion to earn the right to address many of those difficult sub-
jects. But of course, that was part of the reason we decided to
sign on for the long haul.

OPERATION AFRICA

Back in 1960, the majority of the countries on the massive
African continent were under foreign colonial rule. Some
nations, such as Nigeria, were on the cusp of independence,
but many others were hankering for a taste of freedom.
Liberia, a democracy founded by freed American slaves in
the early nineteenth century, was a hopeful exception to the
rule. Still, Liberia aside, the overwhelming sense in the region
was one of political and social unrest.

In some ways, the mood in the air mirrored the one we
knew was brewing back home in the United States. The
American civil rights movement had stirred up a yearning
for justice and given black men and women the hope of full
citizenship in a nation that had long assigned them to
second-class status. That yearning also existed in Africa. And
as in the United States, the push for freedom often started in
the churches.

This is the world I toured in 1957, and I now journeyed
through again in preparation for Billy Graham's arrival.

Billy's Africa crusade began several days before his arrival to the continent. In most large cities or regions, the BGEA crusade strategy often began with several of Billy's associates leading smaller "satellite" meetings in surrounding towns. This approach created buzz and inspired people to invite their friends to the larger crusade, which took place a few days later.

For Billy's tour of Africa, I kicked off the campaign with a week of preaching in Liberia where thousands turned out. The Jones Sisters Trio sang to an enthusiastic response. Billy arrived for the last two days of the week and, by God's Spirit, was often able to "close the deal" with those people who had toyed with the idea of going forward earlier in the week but didn't feel ready. A similar format was employed for Billy's next crusade stop in Ghana. Team evangelist Leighton Ford opened that rally in the capital of Accra and handed off the baton to Billy a day or two later.

Billy's mission to Africa continued through Nigeria and the Congo, Northern and Southern Rhodesia (now Zambia and Zimbabwe), Kenya, Tanganyika (now part of Tanzania), Ruanda-Urundi (now Rwanda and Burundi), Ethiopia, and Egypt. The eight-week tour hit some sixteen cities and drew hundreds of thousands of people—and not a little bit of controversy. In some countries, various groups pressured Billy to speak out on this or that political issue. But through it all, Billy managed to stay on message and focus on the business of proclaiming the gospel to a spiritually hungry land.

NECESSARY INTERRUPTIONS

Before leaving Africa, Billy honored our family by coming to our home to officially dedicate it and us to the work God

had called us to in Liberia. Some three hundred guests attended the ceremony, including President William V. S.
Tubman and Vice President William Tolbert, both professing
Christians. On our patio, which afforded a glorious view of
the ocean, Billy shared a brief message and then prayed over
each member of our family. It was partly a symbolic moment,
but it was also a real transaction between the Lord and His
servants that left us feeling empowered for ministry.

A few weeks later, we were delighted to discover Wanda
was once again pregnant. This time, however, the joy was
mixed with a discernible trace of uneasiness. We wanted to
be in Liberia, but we were not sure how well the next nine
months would go for us in light of the ongoing health con-
cerns that hovered over our family. I had suffered from the
effects of malaria from time to time, and the high fever and
sluggishness seemed to flare up again following my busy
schedule during Billy's crusade across Africa. Wanda had
never adjusted well to the anti-malaria medication we were
all required to take. What's more, there was no telling how
those drugs might affect our unborn child. After much
prayer, and upon the advice of our doctor, we decided to
return to the States—both to strengthen our bodies and to
make sure the impending birth of our newest child would go
smoothly.

We recorded scores of radio programs in advance, packed
only the items we knew we couldn't leave behind, and returned to the United States, where we stayed with my family
in Oberlin. Wanda and I knew it would be difficult to leave
our Monrovia home for at least six months, but we didn't
expect the sorrow displayed by our kids. By God's grace, they
had settled into life in Liberia and genuinely counted it as

home. Perhaps we had to uproot them from the place temporarily to discover just how attached they were to it.

We treated our time in Oberlin almost like a missionary furlough. We enjoyed the relaxed pace for a while and appreciated the time we had to spend with our relatives. My mother and father, in particular, seemed to have aged dramatically since we had left. It was a sharp reminder that time does not suspend itself when we're thousands of miles removed from our loved ones—it ticks on rapidly, and we must play catch-up the best we can while we have the opportunity.

Though we treasured the time with our family in Oberlin, Wanda and I were eager to get back to our ministry in Liberia. With my health improving, Wanda and I decided I would return to Monrovia soon after the birth of the baby along with Gail, Phyllis, and David. Wanda would stay behind with Cheryl and the baby until the doctor gave them the green light to make the long trip. Cheryl, a lovely and precocious girl who would soon be fifteen, could help Wanda with the baby until they rejoined the rest of us in Liberia.

Our dear little Lisa was born three days before Christmas 1960. Her tiny hands gripped my fingers tightly as if she suspected I might be going somewhere. Her sweet little face made me second-guess my plan to return to Africa so quickly. But Wanda assured me that she would be OK and that it was important for us to get back to our responsibilities with ELWA and the BGEA.

So after about six months in the States, Gail, Phyllis, David, and I returned to our home in Monrovia. Three months later we were reunited with Wanda, Cheryl, and Lisa.

The time away, while necessary and recuperative, only reconfirmed our calling to ministry abroad.

FOURTEEN

Breaking Down *More* Barriers

IN PLACES NEAR AND FAR

B illy's tour of Africa was just the beginning of my international service with the Graham Association. In my
thirty-five years with the organization, I toured the United
States and Canada and more than a dozen other countries. I
traveled both alongside Billy and as a solo associate. There
was no shortage of drama wherever I went, whether it was
outbreaks of political uprising (as was the case in Ghana in
1965) or the heartbreaks of racial discrimination (London in
1966 and South Africa in 1973). Through all these travels,
though, I was constantly reminded of two facts that kept me
going despite moments of despondency: the shared sinful-
ness of all humanity and the astounding love of God that
miraculously saves and transforms fallen lives.

After four years of exhilarating ministry in Liberia, a combination of things made it evident that God was calling us
back to the States. My brother, Clarence, who had taken up

our dad's plastering trade, died tragically after a work-related accident in 1962. Since I was scheduled to begin a major crusade in Nigeria the following week, and because the first available flight to the United States was a week away, I regrettably could not make it home for the funeral—a situation that saddens me to this day.

Later Cheryl, Gail, and Phyllis asked if they could attend high school at the Wheaton Christian Academy in Illinois. After praying it through, Wanda and I agreed it would be a good move for the girls; we even escorted them back to the States. However, upon returning to Liberia, Wanda and I almost simultaneously came to the conclusion that our tenure as residents of Africa was coming to a close. In our hearts, we knew we needed to be closer to family—especially with my parents advancing rapidly into old age. What's more, my work with the BGEA afforded me the opportunity to be based anywhere in the world. We realized at this time in our lives it was better for that "anywhere" to be in the United States.

Saying goodbye to our dear friends in Liberia proved to be even more painful the second time around. Nevertheless, this time we knew the work God had called us to do there was complete (at least our small part of it was). We were thankful for the countless people who had come to a saving knowledge of Christ through the ministry of our radio programs, the Bible studies that we hosted in our home, and the regular evangelistic tours that I made throughout the region. We would forever hold a special place in our hearts for the people of Liberia. We knew petitions for their well-being and for the work of ELWA and other missions to Africa would become a permanent fixture on our prayer list.

And my prayers for that war-torn and politically unstable nation continue to this day.

GHANA: CAUGHT IN THE CROSSFIRE

In 1964 we moved back to New York to live again with our dear friend Miss Woolward. When she heard we were returning to the States, she insisted we stay with her. Since those early days at Bethany Church, twenty years earlier, she had moved out of her cozy apartment in the Bronx into a large house in St. Albans, Long Island—just minutes from John F. Kennedy airport. I liked the idea of Wanda and the kids (David, twelve, and Lisa, almost four) living with Miss Woolward, since I would frequently be out of town on business with the BGEA team.

That year a young black seminarian and pastor contacted me about doing an interview for one of his class projects. His name was Ralph Bell and he was a student at Fuller Theological Seminary in Pasadena, California. He had read about me in different places and was interested in writing a scholarly paper about my ministry. I was flattered, of course, but wondered silently whether I had enough ministry under my belt to qualify for term paper status.

When Ralph and I finally met, we hit it off right away. I was at once impressed by his confident but understated demeanor and his ardent passion for evangelism. I invited him to accompany me on a couple of my domestic crusades and gave him some of his first opportunities to preach the gospel before large audiences. He handled those challenges superbly, and after praying about it, I sensed this young man had a special gift. For years, Billy had expressed an interest in adding another black associate to his team. It didn't take me long to realize Ralph would make a strong candidate for such a position. And after he met the BGEA team and participated in a few crusade meetings, everyone believed that Ralph Bell was the man. In 1965 Billy invited him to come on board as an associate, which Ralph gladly accepted.

Later that year, Ralph accompanied me to Ghana for some small evangelistic meetings there. Both Ralph and I preached in villages surrounding the capital, Accra. During one of the meetings, a Southern Baptist missionary approached Ralph and me about going deeper into the interior of the country to preach to some villages in the bush country. I had commitments in Accra that I could not break; yet the invitation seemed like a wonderful opportunity to take the gospel to a needy audience. I asked Ralph if he would be willing to go without me. At first he was hesitant, but after giving it some thought (and some persuasive words from me), Ralph agreed to go. He would rejoin me in Accra the next day. We prayed together and went our separate ways.

I went to bed that evening unaware that one of the most explosive events in Ghana's history was unfolding right outside the walls of my hotel. Early the next morning, I awoke to the radio's news bulletin that a violent coup had taken place in Ghana, and that the nation was in turmoil. A group of rebel soldiers had overthrown the government of Prime Minister Kwame Nkrumah, causing rioting and violent skirmishes in the streets. Nkrumah, who had slowly picked up the reputation of a corrupt and dictatorial leader, had managed to escape. But the country was unstable. All Americans and other foreigners were ordered to stay inside. My first thought was of poor Ralph. I had convinced him to travel into the bush

country for an unscheduled meeting he was not wholeheart-
edly committed to doing. Was he OK? My mind immediately
raced with possible worst-case scenarios. Heaven forbid that
he was caught in some ugly crossfire, or was captured by
rebel soldiers. Finally, though, I rebuked such thoughts and
desperately asked for God's hand of protection over my
young colleague.

Later that day, I had yet to hear anything from Ralph. And
there was little else I could do but continue to seek God on
my friend's behalf.

Another Southern Baptist missionary with whom I was
working arrived at my hotel and coaxed me into keeping a
dinner date at a nearby home. At first I had no intention of
leaving the hotel, but this missionary assured me he knew a
roundabout route that would avoid the potential hotspots.
So I relented, even though I felt the Lord telling me to stay
put.

Sure enough, we were not five minutes from the hotel
before we ran into a roadblock. A handful of armed rebel soldiers approached our car and ordered us to get out. I could
feel my pulse racing, even as I sent prayers up to the Lord.
The soldiers pointed their rifles at us and told us to stand still.
And we obliged, though we probably couldn't have moved
even if we wanted to. In the backseat was a box containing
tracts for our crusade meetings.

"What is in the box?" one of the soldiers demanded.

"Tracts," we told him. But this didn't make sense to him.
So he ordered us to hand him the box. He opened it to find
hundreds of evangelistic pamphlets. The copy on the front
read: "NEW LIFE FOR GHANA!"

"New life for Ghana?" he said. He showed the pamphlets

to the other soldiers. Suddenly, their faces began to soften a bit. "You can go," the soldier finally told us.

We got back in the car, and I insisted that we return to the hotel. This time the missionary concurred.

We were almost back to the hotel when we were stopped again by a different group of soldiers who also ordered us out of the car. These guys seemed a little more intense. They pushed us against the car and patted us down. But as they were doing this, the previous team of soldiers drove by in a truck and yelled to our captors to leave us alone. "They are 'New Life for Ghana' men!" they declared. And the soldiers allowed us to go.

I was thankful to make it back to the hotel without any major incident, but Ralph was still missing in the interior. And the occasional gunshots outside did not help put my mind at ease. But I continued to pray.

A few hours later, after midnight, I heard a knock at my hotel door. I opened it slowly to see Ralph standing there. We immediately hugged and together gave thanks to God.

On his way back to Accra, Ralph also had been held up by rebel soldiers. They detained him for a while, but finally let him go when they realized why he was in the country. It turns out that the resistance forces were all fascinated by this notion of "new life for Ghana." Indeed, the whole reason for the coup was to shake the nation loose of Kwame Nkrumah's oppressive grip. Ralph and I prayed that the rebels and Nkrumah's people alike would come to recognize Jesus Christ as the only lasting key to peace and stability in their nation.

For four days, Ghana was at a standstill. All flights to and from the airport were suspended. The radio stations were taken over by the resistance forces. And Ralph and I were trapped. We learned later that, although Nkrumah escaped, all of his people were either imprisoned or executed.

Things eventually did settle down, and Ralph and I caught a flight home. After a brief stopover in London, we finally made it home.

In my rush to get home, Ralph and I never found a moment to contact our wives to let them know that we were all right and on our way home. So when I finally made it back to New York and rang the doorbell at Miss Woolward's house, Wanda's reaction when she opened the door was one of shock and joy. In fact, she was so happy to see me that she slammed the door in my face.

I kissed and embraced my dear wife for a long, long moment, and then I grabbed each of my kids. It was the best reunion yet! I soon learned how gut-wrenching a wait it was for my family—the phone calls to the BGEA, the State Department, and to Ralph's wife, Jean. Billy actually called at one point to console Wanda, even though he had no idea how we were doing.

With the crisis over, we rejoiced and praised God for His love and protection. But it was hard to shake the visceral feelings of helplessness and peril that confronted Ralph and me in Ghana and our families back home in the United States. Still, it was a timely reminder that the work of the Great Commission brims with dangers as well as blessings.

LONDON: KICKED OUT

A year later, just prior to Billy's London crusade, my blood pressure was sent racing upward again when, because of my skin color, I was told to vacate a London hotel room that the BGEA had booked for me months before. When Billy got wind of this news, he ordered the cancellation of all BGEA's leases for the flat and instructed team members in London to relocate to a facility that did not discriminate according to race. I was able to stay with a friend across town until the BGEA was able to secure new housing for its team members.

The incident made worldwide news. In fact, it was Walter Cronkite's announcement of it on the CBS *Evening News* that first notified Wanda of the matter back home. At first I chalked up the episode as just one more example of racism in the world. But as the week went on, the situation lingered in my head like a bad aftertaste. Even though I knew racial injustice was an ongoing reality in society, that knowledge never lessened the blow of its reality when it hit me personally.

Thankfully, when Billy heard about the situation, he arranged at once for Wanda to join me in London. Having her by my side provided me with a huge emotional boost.

HARLEM: CRUSADE AT THE APOLLO

Despite its low moments, 1966 also was filled with incredible high points. Perhaps my most memorable solo crusade domestically was the Harlem rally at the Apollo Theater. Sponsored by the Harlem Crusade Association, the week-long event drew more than twelve thousand people and a total of one thousand came forward to dedicate their lives to Christ. This was not my biggest crusade; the 1962 meeting in the Congo, which attracted forty thousand people, was my largest and probably most successful meeting internationally. But in the United States, for sheer excitement and energy, none compared to the Harlem event.

As I stood on the stage preaching or singing songs of praise, I was hit at once with the history represented by the Apollo Theater. I was standing where superstars such as Duke Ellington and Count Basie and Sarah Vaughn had performed. As a boy, I had dreamed of one day playing a concert hall such as the Apollo. Now, here I was—God had made my dream a reality. It wasn't exactly as I had envisioned it, but I decided then and there God's version was much better than anything that I had imagined.

The Apollo crusade featured a huge gospel choir directed by a dynamic young Christian named Henry Greenidge. Today Henry pastors the Irvington Covenant Church in Portland, Oregon, but back then he was a sought-after worship director and a student leader with InterVarsity Christian Fellowship. His contribution was immeasurable.

Another major part of the Apollo event was the special music provided by The Jones Sisters Trio. By this time, the girls were twenty-one, nineteen, and seventeen, and they were just reaching the peak of their talents. They had performed at churches across the United States and Africa and were featured at several Billy Graham events. In fact, they had already recorded two albums with Word Records. The Trio's rich, melodic harmonies stirred the crowds, preparing their hearts to receive God's Word. I was proud of them and their commitment to using their gifts to serve the Lord.

Though the Harlem crusade had drawn good numbers, it probably would have drawn even more had we enjoyed the widespread support of white ministers in the New York area. While several black churches worked with us to promote the event, several of the white church leaders we approached explained that they were too busy to help us with the crusade. One shining exception was my friend Dr. Stephen Olford, who is today recognized as a champion of expository preaching. Back then he was renowned as the senior pastor of Calvary Baptist Church in New York City. Stephen did all he could to get the word out about the event, and he was the featured preacher one of the evenings.

A book's worth of poignant testimonies came as a result of the Harlem event, but one woman's story stands out to me. This woman, whom I'll call Rhonda, had killed her husband after she discovered he had cheated on her. Rhonda served a ten-year prison sentence and was released just before the start of the Harlem crusade.

Rhonda had paid the penalty for her crime and was now a free woman—except she wasn't free inside. She fell into a deep depression and decided that she would commit suicide. But one night as she walked down 125th Street in Harlem, she saw the marquee lights at the Apollo Theater, and she read some of the words on the sign: CRUSADE. FREE. HOPE. GOD. As she drew closer to the theater, she could hear the exuberant voices of the choir singing inside. Moved by their joyful spirit, she took a deep breath and went inside. The place was packed, but Rhonda found a seat just in time to hear me come to the stage. That night I preached on the power of the Cross. I told the crowd about how Jesus had left heaven to enter a sin-cursed world where He lived among men and women to show them a better way. "On the cross," I said, "Jesus bore all of our sins—every one of them! I don't care what sin you've committed today—adultery, greed, murder, pridefulness. Whatever it is, Jesus bore it on the cross. He died to liberate us from the bondage of those sins."

Rhonda listened carefully and when the invitation to come forward was extended, she stood to her feet and dashed to the foot of the stage. "This was the night that I was going to take my life," she later told a counselor. "But it became the night that I *found* life."

The testimonies that sprung out of the Harlem crusade reminded me that the gospel is not some pie-in-the-sky prescription for going to heaven. No, it is much more than that. The gospel is a *now* message for redeeming, restoring, and rebuilding broken lives. Andraé Crouch's classic chorus would later proclaim "Jesus is the answer for the world *today* . . ." And I couldn't agree more.

Yes, God wants us to repent and turn our lives over to Him so we can spend eternity in heaven. But He also has something for us right now. We don't have to wait until heaven to experience God's peace and joy and transforming power. He gives us His Holy Spirit the moment we believe in Him, and from that moment on we are beneficiaries of His abundant life. It may not mean that we get rich or that we get out of jail or that we escape the immediate consequences for the sinful things we've done. However, it does mean God has taken control of our lives, and He will walk with us and give us strength and grace for whatever circumstances we must face. Time and again, I saw people in Harlem whose futures were revolutionized the moment they grasped this simple but amazing good news.

Throughout the remainder of the '60s and into the '70s, I was privileged to lead many crusades at locations across the United States. My weekly radio ministry—which was by this time known as the *Hour of Freedom*—also continued to grow during this period. Even today, I run into people who tell me stories of how their lives were transformed from listening to our radio broadcasts. One Air Force pilot was flying over South America one day in the early '70s when he picked up our broadcast on his radio. What a joy it was to hear the gospel explained so clearly at 37,000 feet in the air, he told me years later. I also received a lot of letters from prison inmates who listened to the broadcast or who were inspired to ask Christ into their hearts after I preached at their facilities in person, which I tried to do on a regular basis at prisons throughout the country.

SOUTH AFRICA: STANDING FIRM

Probably one of the most controversial crusade stops for Billy was his 1973 campaign in South Africa, then a hotbed of legislated racism. The popular term for the country's ugly brand of discrimination, of course, was *apartheid*.

For years, South African church leaders had beseeched Billy to do a crusade in their nation, but Billy refused to come unless they could promise him the meetings would be integrated and that his integrated team of associates would be welcomed. Church leaders backed off when they realized there was no way to lawfully meet Billy's demands.

By 1972 things had begun to change. A group of evangelicals in South Africa invited Billy to speak at a special conference on evangelism. The BGEA informed them that Billy's requirement that the event be racially integrated still stood, but this time the churches and the government agreed to meet his demands.

So in March 1973 the South African Congress on Mission and Evangelism convened in the coastal resort city of

Durban. It was a fully integrated affair with some seven hundred Christian leaders of all races and Protestant persuasions.

There was also a fully integrated evangelistic rally in Durban where more than 45,000 people (half of them nonwhite) gathered to hear the gospel proclaimed. More than 3,000 people came forward during the invitation. That meeting was followed a week later by an even bigger rally in Johannesburg. That event attracted a diverse audience of 60,000, and more than 4,000 people streamed forward to accept Christ.

It was a historic ten days. Many people remarked that it was the largest interracial event held in South Africa to that date. Zulu music mixed with European-style gospel tunes to create a rich mosaic of praise and worship. Billy's challenge to the crowds was bold and blunt: "Christianity is not a white man's religion, and don't let anybody ever tell you it's white or black. Christ belongs to all people!"

I had the opportunity to speak at a satellite meeting held at a Dutch Reformed Church in Durban. It was an Afrikaners congregation brimming with white faces. Though I was a bit nervous at first—given the social and historical context of the country—I felt the Holy Spirit speaking through me that day. I spoke frankly about the gospel of freedom and grace and that there is now neither Jew nor Greek, slave nor free in Christ Jesus. Afterward, an Afrikaner came up to me and said, "You're the first black man to preach from that pulpit. I never thought a black man could preach like that." I smiled and chose to take it as a compliment.

Though we challenged South Africa's racial status quo left and right during our evangelistic events, it was clear that, outside the imported tolerance and evangelical atmosphere at the stadiums and conference hall, it was business as usual in

the streets of the nation. Yes, the hotel that we stayed in
agreed to accommodate both blacks and whites. However,
outside those walls the spirit of segregation prevailed.

Whites, for instance, were the only ones who could stroll
the white sands of Durban's beautiful beaches; mixed race
and black persons were restricted to the less pristine stretches
of the seashore.

A handful of us from the BGEA team got an up close look
at the country's structures when on two occasions we attempted to pick up a late-night meal at local eateries. The
first time, we tried to dine at a restaurant that displayed a
"Whites Only" sign in its window. They refused to serve us
(or, more specifically, me). So we decided to keep looking
until we found a restaurant that served both blacks and
whites. After nearly an hour of driving around the city, I told
the men with me to go ahead and get something to eat without me. Instead, we ended up buying fast food and eating it
on the side of the road. "I'm so sorry, Howard," my colleague
Leighton Ford said to me. "I've never seen anything like this
before."

A few days later, in a different part of the country, we again
searched for a late-night meal. We found a diner that didn't
display a sign in the window, but once we walked through
the door we realized it was run by blacks. The patrons stared
at us for a long, uncomfortable time before the owner finally
explained that I was welcome there but my associates would
have to leave.

Later, Leighton chatted with me again about what had
happened that evening. "Howard," he said, "now I know how
you must feel sometimes—not only in this country but back
in the States as well."

Since those days, much has happened in South Africa to move it away from its system of *apartheid* and into a more just and humane structure. Power has been restored to the black citizens, and the country has slowly started down a path toward reconciliation. Obviously, both blacks and whites have a long way to go there. But it's heartening that some progress has been made.

I like to think our meetings there thirty years ago played some small role in nudging the nation toward racial healing. I pray God will continue to break down that nation's barriers—both those in the political structures and those in the hearts of men.

PART FIVE

Looking Back—and Ahead

FIFTEEN

Family Matters
LIVING, LOVING, AND REMEMBERING

One afternoon in Monrovia, when our son David, was seven, he came storming into the house with what he clearly felt was exciting news.

"Mommy! Daddy! Guess what Jimmy and I did!"

At this point, we had been back in Liberia for less than a year, but David already had become best chums with little Jimmy, another missionary kid. The pair found all sorts of "boy" things to do in their adopted land—skipping stones off the ocean surface, capturing and then releasing strange bugs, playing makeshift games of baseball on the beach. They were generally good boys. Nevertheless, they were *boys*. Translation: They conjured up their fair share of mischief, for instance on this day. At first, David's unbridled excitement failed to raise our suspicions. But that didn't last long.

"What did you and Jimmy do?" Wanda quietly answered David.

"We went preaching! In the village!"

"You did what?" I quickly said, beating Wanda to the punch. The first part of David's statement wasn't so bad. After all, he was the son of a preacher. David had shown a penchant for preaching since his toddler years, when he would stand on a stool and mimic his daddy's pulpit gestures in front of an imaginary congregation. And since both Wanda and I encouraged him—and all our kids—to read their Bibles and to, in the apostle Paul's words, "be ready in season and out" to share the good news of their faith, it was only natural for him to dabble in the family business.

What was troubling was the second half of David's announcement—"In the village." I had repeatedly warned the boy that he was not to go into the interior village without an adult accompanying him. "Now David, you know you're not supposed to go into the village without permission," I said in my best stern-but-patient disciplinarian voice.

"I know, Daddy, but I was 'passing the Word.'"

Wanda and I shot quick glances at each other. *Passing the Word* was the Liberian phrase used to describe the preaching of the gospel.

David continued: "And Daddy, we even took up an offering!" He dipped his hand into his pocket and pulled it out to produce a fistful of pennies. Wanda and I stared at each other in disbelief. The wonderful humor of the moment was not lost on us. Yet, at the same time, we had to present a convincing demeanor of parental concern and displeasure with what our son had done. Those villagers had nothing to spare, yet they had given their money to David and Jimmy. They had truly sacrificed.

By now, David was beginning to understand that we did not share in his enthusiasm over his little evangelistic outing in the village. But we tried to remain calm as we walked him through a review of his actions.

"Tell me exactly what happened in the village, son," I said.

"We went to the village, and I stood on a box and preached while Jimmy handed out tracts."

"What did you preach about?"

"I told the people about John 3:16—'For God so loved the world that he gave his only begotten Son, that whosoever believeth in him should not perish but have everlasting life.' I told them that if they loved Jesus and believed on Him they would go to heaven, but if they didn't love Jesus, they would be lost. Some of them raised their hands to accept Jesus, and then we took an offering." (David later told me that an offering is what he presumed all preachers did following their sermons.)

David added that the villagers encouraged Jimmy and him to come back soon. "Daddy, please don't be mad. We were 'passing the Word.'"

"David," I said, squeezing back my amusement, "you disobeyed us by going into the village without an adult. I'm glad that you want to tell people about Jesus, but don't ever go into that village again without Mommy, me, or another grownup that we trust."

David nodded sweetly.

"And as far as taking an offering goes, son—believe it or not, you actually can tell people about the Lord without taking up a collection." I finally let loose an audible chuckle, and Wanda and David joined in. "Here's what you're going to do," I continued. "Take that money to the ELWA station, and give it to Aunt Clara. She'll know how to use it to help the people." ("Aunt Clara," as she was known to all the children, was a Liberian woman who worked at ELWA and was an in-fluential force in getting the locals out to ministry events.)

With that, David dashed out the door. And I stood there, feeling a combination of amusement and fatherly pride. That day, Wanda and I knew without a doubt that we had a future preacher on our hands.

"PASSING THE WORD"

David's little preaching escapade was a lighthearted ex-ample of what Wanda and I made sure the whole family did while we lived in Monrovia. We all had an obligation to pass the Word. We were not just there to enjoy the balmy weather and beautiful beach. Everyday ministry—beyond my preach-ing tours and Wanda's and my radio broadcasts—was a cen-tral part of the Jones family's life. I believed it was essential that we get out and live among the people of our adopted home. For many American missionaries, the temptation was great to broadcast the gospel message to the African people but to avoid personal contact. I did not want our family to fall into that trap.

So on Sunday afternoons, Cheryl, Gail, and Phyllis would go into the villages to share Bible stories and teach praise songs to the local children. The Liberian kids adored the col-orful flannel-graph boards the girls would use to present the stories. In addition, the girls—in their role as The Jones Sis-ters Trio—sang in local churches, on the radio, and provided special music for several of my crusade events.

Wanda, who continued to blossom as a speaker in her own right, spoke to numerous women's groups throughout Liberia and developed a reputation as a thoughtful and passionate woman of God. A particularly thrilling moment for Wanda was an invitation from the Council of Evangelical Women in Nigeria to travel through the interior on a five-week tour that allowed her to speak to five thousand women. In many locations on the tour, Wanda was the first black American woman ever to address an audience there.

Wanda and I also felt a special obligation to reach out to the handful of black American missionaries sprinkled throughout Monrovia and the more rural interior areas of Liberia—people like Wilfred and Betty Quimby (also mentioned in chapter 10). More than any other African nation, Liberia attracted black American missionaries—primarily because it was one of the few African countries with an open-door policy on missions. We felt called to provide encouragement and support to the black missionaries at the Killingsworth Mission and others. After all, we knew first hand how lonely a road it could be to be black trailblazers in the predominantly white evangelical world of ministry.

One of the surprise blessings that arose out of our work in Liberia was the birth of the Monrovia Bible Institute. During our first trip to Africa in 1957, we preached a massive one-week crusade at the Executive Pavilion in Monrovia. By week's end, more than six hundred people had come forward to dedicate their lives to Christ. Present at that event was Naomi Doles, a young and fiery African-American woman. She was a new missionary with the Carver Foreign Missions Board, based in Atlanta, Georgia. Naomi had come to Liberia to work with young people, and she was instrumental in helping to launch the Liberian branch of Youth for Christ. She also worked with ELWA on weekends.

Naomi and others from Carver spent a lot of their time

ministering to many of the people who had become Christians through my preaching at those early meetings in 1957. Soon, the Carver contingent saw a need for starting a Bible school to help nurture the young faith of all those converts—hence the founding of the Monrovia Bible Institute. When Wanda and I learned of this work upon our return to Liberia, we dedicated ourselves to helping however we could, usually by coming in to speak to the students.

As the school grew, additional Carver missionaries were sent to teach and assist the effort. Many of these young missionaries grew close to our family. In addition to Naomi, women like Coral McCleery, Mary Stevens, and Henrietta Herron became dear friends who also served as fine role models (and occasional caretakers) for our children.

In time, it became evident that the Bible school would need a permanent facility to house its swelling numbers. After speaking to Naomi and Cora, I decided to speak to President Tubman about obtaining land on which a school could be built. After listening to my appeal, President Tubman decided to donate twenty-three acres of land—located right across the road from ELWA—to the project. With generous support from Carver and other mission groups, the building was completed and the Monrovia Bible Institute had its new home. I was honored when the Carver organization invited me to serve as the school's first president, which I did until we left Liberia in 1962.

CIRCLE OF LIFE

As I described earlier, the reason we eventually left our Liberian home was because of family—and our sense God was directing us to return to the United States.

After spending our first few years back in the United States living with Miss Woolward in New York, Wanda and I discovered my dad's health had deteriorated and my mom, whose strength had been diminished by old age, was struggling to care for him. We knew we were needed back home in Oberlin. So, in 1965 we made the trip westward.

Moving our family into my childhood home in Oberlin felt like coming full circle. Mom and Dad were thrilled to have us with them, even though it meant getting used to additional bodies scurrying around the house. David and his grandfather became fast friends; and Dad fell equally hard for his precious little granddaughter Lisa. We enjoyed a tremendous time of quality bonding, and everything seemed bright and cheery—until the doctors revealed the heart-wrenching news: Dad was suffering from leukemia and would not have much more time on this earth.

We prayed for God's will to be done, and we took advantage of the time we had left. When he felt up to it, Dad never missed a chance to go out to the ball field to watch David play Little League. We squeezed as much joy and affection as we could out of the remaining time, but soon, on November 19, 1967, Dad went home to be with the Lord.

Right about now, you're probably wondering what happened to that stubborn, rough-edged man who ranted against my going to Nyack to become a minister. Well, I should tell you that over the years the prayers of family and friends, along with the standard issues of life, conspired to draw my dad closer to the Lord. In fact, the man who once refused to give me any money to go to Nyack later paid for Wanda to accompany me on my first trip to Africa. Indeed, during the last years of Dad's life, he mellowed a bit. He listened to the radio all the time, and the dial was always tuned to the local Moody station. Before he finally passed away, he called me to his bedside and told me, "Son, it's all right now." I knew what he meant. Perhaps the greatest heritage a parent can leave his loved ones is the peace and assurance that his soul is in good hands.

Seeing my mom's health take a turn for the worse a decade later might have been even harder than watching Dad's decline, since Mom had always been an indomitable force. However, a series of strokes left her body weakened and partially paralyzed. So after much prayer and internal wrestling, Wanda and I felt we had no choice but to place her in a nearby nursing home. We visited her daily, as did members from our church. But we were left with an incredible sadness. A few months later, on June 6, 1976, she went home to the Lord. It is so painful to watch a loved one disappear before your eyes. And little did I know, Mom's situation was only the beginning.

As I look back, I am grateful for the good, quality time we were able to spend with Mom and Dad—and especially that our kids were able to know and love them as well, since Wanda's parents had passed away before they could meet any of their grandchildren.

THE "CHURCH BABIES" GROW UP

Had Wanda's parents lived to see their grandchildren, they would have been as proud and delighted over those precious little people as I am today over the adult versions. Wanda and I always prayed that God would ultimately guide our children to a personal faith in Christ. While we saw each of them make commitments to the Lord as children, it was even more encouraging to seem them take that faith with them as they matured into adulthood. Today, I'm able to look at each of them and see God's faithfulness in answering prayers. As they lead their own families in the way of the Lord, I continue to seek God's covering of love and protection over their futures.

Cheryl, who is married to Norman Sanders (an ordained minister who directs communications at the Billy Graham Training Center at the Cove in Asheville, North Carolina), has two grown sons. She is a Bible teacher and frequently speaks to women's groups. She continues to share her musical gifts as a church soloist. Cheryl, whose dynamic Bible studies draw upwards of thirty women each week, tells me her most outrageous memory from childhood was accidentally falling into a lake with all her clothes and shoes on at a youth camp in New York. She remembers I had to fish her out. I'm glad I did.

After a brief career as a flight attendant with United Airlines, Gail married Andre Thornton, who was a professional baseball player with the Cleveland Indians before starting his own consulting business, Global Promotions and Incentives. Andre is also a trustee at Nyack College. Gail and Andre have three grown sons and live outside Cleveland. "The Jones kids were affectionately called 'church babies,'" Gail recalls, "because being in church on Sunday morning, sometimes Sunday afternoon, and then back again on Sunday evening made for long days—and that doesn't even include Wednesday prayer service, Saturday youth group, and the occasional all-night prayer meeting." Still, she says, she loved it. Today, when Gail is not assisting her husband, she continues to use her musical gifts to share the gospel.

Phyllis also worked briefly as a flight attendant. Then she, too, married a professional ballplayer—Pat Kelly, who played with the Baltimore Orioles. Today, Pat is an evangelist with Life Line Ministries; he and Phyllis have one teenage daughter and live in Timonium, Maryland. "Something that has left a real impression on me is the fact that Mom never complained when you were away," Phyllis recently told me. "She knew evangelism was what God had called you to do, and she was supportive of it. Now that I'm married to an evangelist, I know it had to be tough on Mom at times. But she never let us know it. She kept the household running and did a great job." Amen.

My only son, David—or H. David Jones—is married to a wonderful woman named Daphne and has three grown stepchildren. He lives in Seattle, where he is an elementary school counselor and the founder of a ministry called Father Matters. A graduate of Gordon-Conwell Seminary, David has pastored Alliance churches in Michigan and Ohio and continues to write and perform gospel music. He tells me one of his favorite memories from childhood was the day in Monrovia when we entered the father-son kite-flying contest at the last minute, using a makeshift kite that was quickly assembled from sticks, rope, and a piece of his mother's tablecloth. We won the contest and my nine-year-old boy just cried and cried. The first prize, David recalls, was a huge chocolate bar. But he says the best part was spending that time together. I couldn't agree more.

Lisa, married to Michael McGloiry, lives in Los Angeles and has two teenage step-sons. She graduated from Ohio

State University with a degree in music and recently went back to school to pursue a law degree. She works as a project manager for an international consulting firm. Lisa recalls one of the funniest moments from her youth was the day she and her mother prayed for her dog, Muffy, after he suddenly took ill. Unbeknownst to Wanda, Lisa had taken the anointing oil that I had brought back from one of my trips to the Holy Land and poured it on Muffy while they prayed. (I was out of town when this happened.) When Wanda opened her eyes to see Muffy drenched in holy oil, she almost pitched a fit. On the bright side, Muffy started feeling better. Lisa, however, would think twice before "borrowing" Daddy's things. Still, no one could accuse my little girl of lacking faith. She recently told me: "One thing I really appreciated about our family was that it didn't matter if you were human or canine—we were taught that 'prayer changes things.'" As for my anointing oil: Lisa and Wanda didn't tell me about their little healing service until many years later. In the meantime, they refilled my little white vase with Wesson cooking oil.

I give thanks to God every day for the way that He has taken care of my family. Perhaps the single greatest regret about my career is the time that it took away from my family. Though I knew God had called me to preach His Word around the world, it never made leaving home any easier. I'm just grateful the heavenly Father was always there, even when this earthly one wasn't. How glad I am that those adorable "church babies" went on to become "church grownups" who love the Lord.

SIXTEEN

Losing Wanda
THE LONGEST GOOD-BYE

Yes, too much time away from home was the biggest regret of my ministry. But the biggest regret of my life was that, when all the globetrotting and relentless activity was over, I was not able to spend these twilight years with my beloved wife.

In 1990 Wanda became ill. Around that time, I had a weeklong crusade in central Wisconsin. Wanda was there with me, along with Walter Grist, my crusade director; his wife, Jeneva, (who was a wonderful soloist); our pianist Eddie Thomas; and Steve Musto (another stellar soloist).

One morning, Wanda and Jeneva left to attend a large gathering of women. The event was an offshoot of my crusade. Wanda was the featured speaker. Since it was a "ladies only" event, I stayed at the hotel to work on my message for that evening.

About three hours later, Wanda and Jeneva returned to the hotel, and Jeneva informed me in a calm but concerned voice that Wanda had not been feeling well. "What was the trouble?" I asked.

"I don't know, Howard," Jeneva said. "Wanda delivered a great message. The women were blessed by it. But after she got through speaking, she had a vomiting spell."

I could look at Wanda and tell she wasn't herself. I told her, "I'm glad you're back." But she seemed to be in a haze.

I took her to the local hospital. The attending doctor examined her thoroughly then said, "There's something serious here." After consulting with other doctors, he told me, "Reverend Jones, you should get your wife back to Ohio as soon as possible."

I couldn't just cancel the crusade, so I asked Walter if he would deliver the message for the remaining two nights. "Don't worry, Howard," he said. "We'll finish off the crusade."

So Wanda and I got on the plane and headed home to Ohio. I prayed, "Lord, please take care of my precious wife." On the plane we were holding hands, and she looked at me. She said, "Howard, where are you?"

"I'm right here, honey," I said.

"I can't see you."

"What? You can't see me?"

"No." Then after a moment she said, "Oh, now I see you."

Needless to say, I was getting more nervous by the minute. *Something is seriously wrong here*, I said to myself.

When we finally arrived in Cleveland, Reverend Charles Mayle, our pastor at the Oberlin Alliance Church, met us and took us directly to the hospital. The doctor examined her, and came to me with a solemn expression on his face. "It looks as if she's had a stroke," he said. "We'll have to keep her here for a few days to monitor her condition."

Two days later, the phone rang at our house. It was the doctor calling to inform me that Wanda would need surgery right away to stop bleeding that they had discovered on her brain. I gave my consent, and alerted our family and friends. Finally, when all the calls were made, I dropped to my knees. "Oh, Lord," I said. "I know that Wanda is in Your hands. Please guide those surgeons as they operate."

Suddenly, while I was kneeling there by the living room window, I looked up to see a big, white dove land on our porch. We saw lots of doves in our area, but none of them were ever as large as this one. He just strolled around our porch nonchalantly before taking off again into the air. Enthralled, I watched the white bird fly away.

While I was contemplating this rather strange phenomenon, it seemed as though the Lord was saying to me, *Howard, you know the dove in Scripture is a sign of peace and the Holy Spirit*. And that knowledge gave me peace. "Lord," I said, "You must have sent that dove there just to quiet my nerves and let me know that Wanda would be all right."

HOLDING ON FOR LIFE

Over the next several days, we received cards and calls from countless folks who let us know that they were praying for us. A particularly special call came right before Wanda was to go into surgery. "Howard," the caller said, "this is Billy Graham. Did I hear that Wanda is in the hospital?"

"Yes, she's going into surgery any minute now," I told Billy. He asked about the surgeon, whether I was satisfied with his credentials. I told him he was supposed to be the best in the county, so we were trusting God that he'd do a great job. Then Billy asked if he could pray for me right there over the telephone lines. And we did. It felt good to know a man as busy and important as Billy took time to minister to one of his associates.

This, of course, was not the first time Billy had gone out of his way to show his love and support for Wanda and me. When we made Liberia our permanent home in 1959, Billy made it a point to build time into his packed tour of Africa to stop by our house in Monrovia to dedicate it. Then, about thirty-four years ago, Billy made a trip to Oberlin to honor Wanda and me on the occasion of our twenty-fifth wedding anniversary. While in town, he made a stop at the newly renovated Murray Ridge Center, a school for the mentally challenged, where Wanda faithfully worked as a teacher for some thirteen years after we resettled in Oberlin. Billy's appearance in Ohio, though not connected with any larger crusade event, made front-page news in the area papers.

As word of Wanda's illness spread, other calls came—from Cliff Barrows, Ruth Bell Graham, and many others with whom we had co-labored throughout the years. We had loads of prayer support, and it helped our family through those moments of uncertainty.

After nearly five hours, the surgery was complete. The doctors declared it a success, and Wanda was allowed to come home after about a week of rest in the hospital.

The surgeons had shaved off all of Wanda's beautiful black locks, so when the hair eventually started to return, it was a striking white. But even though my wife had a "new look," she was still my woman, and I was glad to have her back home.

Her recovery seemed to go incredibly smoothly. When I took her back to the hospital for follow-up visits, the doctors were amazed at how she seemed to be rallying after such a major operation.

For a while, things were back to normal. Wanda returned to her speaking ministry, and the two of us worked together on the book *Heritage and Hope: The Legacy and Future of the Black Family in America*. Wanda also made contributions to a women's study Bible. But a year or so later, She began complaining again about not feeling well. And soon she started exhibiting signs of forgetfulness. Names of family and friends would escape her, and several times she forgot to take her medication.

Oh, Lord, I hope this isn't too serious, I said to myself. But deep inside, I knew things would likely never be the same again.

The thing that drove home the reality of our new situation was how she'd frequently start cooking in the kitchen then forget how many place settings to prepare at the table. One night we were going to have steaks and it was just the two of us, but she brought three steaks from the refrigerator. "It's just you and me, Babe," I'd tell her.

On another occasion, she was fixing supper again, and all of a sudden she said, "I want to ask you a question."

"Yes, dear," I said. "What is it?"

"Where's my husband?"

"What do you mean? I'm right here."

"No. No. Where is my husband, Howard?" she demanded again, this time with more urgency. "I haven't seen him. Where is he?"

I said, "*I'm* your husband." But she would not accept it.

"You know you're not my husband. Clarence is my husband."

"Wanda, Clarence has been dead for years. I'm your husband."

She thought about this a moment, then finally shook her head. "Well, have it your way," she said, as if to appease me.

There was no doubt in my mind: We were in serious trouble. And then it got worse. Wanda began walking off from the house by herself. I'd go outside searching but couldn't find her. So I'd get in the car and drive around town. I'd spot her walking through the college campus. I'd honk the horn. She'd come over to the car, and I'd ask her, "What are you doing?"

"I decided to take a walk. Can't I take a walk?" Sometimes in these moments she'd get a bit feisty and argumentative, so I'd walk with her until she was ready to go home.

Another time she left the house in the evening during a rainstorm. It was pouring outside, and all she had on was a nightgown and slippers. When these episodes occurred, I'd often get a phone call from a friend or relative who had taken Wanda into their home.

The final straw came one day when David was home for the weekend. Wanda, who had always been a wonderful cook, was in the kitchen preparing a meal, when suddenly she called for me. When I got there, I found her on the floor, shaking in a seizure like manner. I called David, who at once telephoned for an ambulance.

After extensive testing, the doctors came to the conclusion that Wanda was suffering from a form of dementia that would likely progress into a full-blown case of Alzheimer's disease. They told me I might eventually need to put Wanda into a nursing home, but I didn't want to hear that. I couldn't bring myself to accept it.

Ultimately I did accept it. And I watched as my dear wife slowly slipped into a world that was farther and farther away from this reality.

PREACHING TO MYSELF

From the day we admitted Wanda to the nursing home, I visited her once and often two or three times per day. (Coincidentally, both Wanda's sister Ruth and brother Alden were also residents at the home. Ruth passed away in 2000 at 85; Alden, 91, is still there today.) Early on, Wanda seemed to look forward to our time together. She'd wave to me out the big bay window when she'd see me arriving. But in time, her expressions grew increasingly blank. Some days were better than others. But for the most part, Wanda was losing her handle on who I was.

Wanda had never resisted going to a nursing home. She knew something was wrong. And she told me, "Whatever you have to do, you have to do; the Lord will take care of me. I know you love me. Don't worry."

But I *did* worry. And I talked to God constantly about this troubling new state of affairs. The heart of my prayers to Him was—and sometimes still is—*Why?*

There were times when I wept uncontrollably. There are times even now that I look at her picture and think about what we've lost. I think about the marriage we had. She was the greatest wife any man could have. And many times I sit here in this lovely home the Lord has provided and say, "Lord, why have You allowed me to be here by myself at this stage in my life?" Or, in other words, "Why have You forsaken me? Did I do something? Was there something I did or didn't do that You're punishing me for, taking my wife away from me?"

But then I go to the Word and open up a lot of passages that I read aloud to myself. Almost anything in the Psalms brings comfort and peace. I also run to 2 Corinthians 4, where Paul says: "Therefore, since through God's mercy we have this ministry, we do not lose heart. . . . We are hard pressed on every side, but not crushed; perplexed, but not in despair; persecuted, but not abandoned; struck down, but not destroyed" (vv. 1, 8-9). And of course, Romans 8:28—"In all things God works for the good of those who love him"— has brought many moments of understanding and relief.

God also reminded me of the numerous sermons I have preached on death, loss, grief, and the hope of the resurrection. It was akin to the time when I was in Ghana in 1957. I was so nervous and worried, and the Lord said, "You just closed a great crusade, and you preached to these people about trusting Me. Now go back and preach some of your sermons to yourself. You've given stuff out; now you take it." And that is what I've striven to do.

As Christians, we often want everything smooth. But the Christian life is not an easy one. When we get saved, in that moment, we're enrolled in the School of the Cross; family problems, financial problems, the loss of loved ones. Contrary to what some preachers have been peddling lately, Christians are not immune to any of these things. We are, however, promised grace and strength to walk through the conflict.

At times, I've been able to look at the bright side of Wanda's illness. Going to the nursing home every day gave me the opportunity to reach out to several nurses and even some of the other residents. Often a warm smile, or a quick hello is all it takes to bless someone's day at the home. I also had the opportunity to hand out copies of Wanda's inspiring autobiography, *Living in Two Worlds.* First published in 1988, the book describes the miraculous ways that God worked in her life—not to mention the life of the Jones family—to help us take the gospel to the entire world. Though Wanda's mind and voice had been silenced, her ministry lived on through her book.

Seeing Wanda's condition worsen was more difficult than watching my mother's decline. Here again a once-energetic, strong-willed woman was stripped of all the vigor and passion that had made her an indomitable force for God. Yet I knew the soul of my beloved Wanda was still there, trapped in a broken and feeble shell of flesh.

In the mornings, before I set out to see her at the nursing home, I would pray that God would continue to fill her with His life and love. One morning, I said, "Now, Lord, I'm praying for her. Even though she cannot physically pray anymore, You still know all the prayers that Wanda has prayed during her lifetime—all the prayers she prayed before I met her and all the prayers we prayed together; the times we fasted and prayed, and I took my turn praying and then she chimed in; the times we'd pray together before going out on the road; the prayers she would send up to You during personal devotion time—all those prayers have gone up before You. Now she can't pray, but You just reactivate those prayers. Just reactivate that lifetime of prayers." Wanda was a praying woman, and I imagine that, even though I couldn't see it, she was still offering up prayers in her incapacitated state.

Many wonderful friends and family members came by to visit on those long days prior to Wanda's passing. Ruth's daughter, Sondra Hodge, who lives in Oberlin, was a frequent visitor. Alden's son Danny Young and his wife, Susan, and their two children also dropped in regularly. My sister-in-law Helen Jones (Clarence's widow) was always a great encouragement, as was her daughter (and my niece) Diane "Pepper" Poyer. The two of them drove in from Wheaton, Illinois, on several occasions to see "Aunt Wanda."

Though she was usually lost in the fog of Alzheimer's, there were many wonderful moments of lucidity when we saw flashes of our beloved Wanda. From time to time, I would bring her home for a change of scenery. In 2000, Wanda was sitting at home with Cheryl, Gail, and Lisa by her side. Cheryl and Gail began to sing the hymn "Give Me Jesus," one of Wanda's favorites. But it was too much for precious Lisa. She began to cry. As her eyes moistened, Wanda suddenly reached over and, with a smile, lovingly wiped away her daughter's tears.

On another occasion, as she sat with David, she gently pointed to her head and said, "David, I'm not wired right anymore." The message was unmistakable: she wanted to communicate but couldn't.

Patricia Young, a local poet and friend of our family, made regular visits to the nursing home. Wanda always seemed to be buoyed by her presence. About a month before Wanda's passing, Patricia popped in for a visit. But this time, Patricia recalls, Wanda seemed distant. Patricia read to her as usual, but Wanda just stared out the window. She seemed preoccupied by the sunlight. Looking back on that day, Patricia believes Wanda was simply preparing for her imminent journey. Soon she would be in the light of God's everlasting presence.

LEGACY OF FAITH

Wanda died at the Allen Memorial Hospital in Oberlin on November 8, 2001. A beautiful and devoted wife and mother, she left behind a deep and immeasurable legacy of faith that has impacted countless souls for eternity—including this one.

For several days prior to her passing, Wanda hadn't been feeling well. The doctors admitted her to the Intensive Care Unit at the hospital and began administering oxygen. Gail, Reverend and Mrs. Mayle, Maurice Shave, and a few others gathered with me at the hospital. We would learn later that Wanda had suffered a mild heart attack. In one disturbing moment, the doctors asked the family whether we wanted them to take heroic measures to preserve Wanda's life. Trusting that God would take care of Wanda in His own way, we refused.

As it turns out, heroic measures were not necessary. Wanda pulled through, and the next day she enjoyed a wonderful time of fellowship with family and friends.

Wanda flashed a warm smile as she saw everyone surrounding her. I asked her if she knew these people, and she said, "Yes, I know them." She beamed when she saw Gail and Pastor's Mayle's wife, Mary.

We stayed at the hospital for the entire morning, laughing, reminiscing, and praying. Soon, however, we decided to leave for a while and allow Wanda to get some needed rest. I said a quiet prayer and kissed her goodbye. "I'll be back a little later," I told her.

But a few hours later, a call came from the hospital. "Reverend Jones," the doctor said, "I'm sorry to inform you that Mrs. Jones died a few minutes ago. She passed away peacefully in her sleep."

I hung up the phone and immediately went to pieces. Right then and there, the Lord and I had it out. "Why God?" I cried. "Why didn't you let me see her a last time?" I was especially grieved that I wasn't at Wanda's bedside, holding her hand when the Lord called her home. But Gail helped me put things in perspective. "Dad," she said, "you need to remember the happy times. We should be thankful that we got to spend the morning with her, and that she was so happy."

People came from all over town—and across the nation— to attend Wanda's memorial services. At the conclusion of the wake, David called the members of the immediate family together for one last look at the body that once held our dear wife and mother. We prayed, thanking God for the gift of her life and imploring Him to keep her legacy alive in our hearts and various ministries.

The next day, at the funeral, Ralph Bell offered the invocation and shared some personal remarks; Cheryl and David offered poignant reflections; Reverend Mayle delivered the eulogy; and Cheryl's husband, Norman Sanders, closed in prayer. One of the hymns we sang that morning was "All the Way My Savior Leads Me," which was a song we used to sing as a duet. It was one of the themes of our life together.

At a graveside service, conducted by Norman, we assembled to say one final good-bye. The November air was bitterly cold that day—cemeteries are cold anyway—but the warmth of my love for my dear wife made me oblivious to the morning chill. Wanda was absent from the body, but her soul was with the Lord. She had just changed addresses. I knew in my heart that I would see her again. As the tears fell that morning, they were not so much from the burden of grief as from thankful hearts for a life well lived.

I still weep sometimes. The kids weep, too. But we know there was a purpose in Wanda's suffering. There is purpose and meaning in all of our sufferings when we know the Lord.

One positive thing that has come out of this ordeal is my participation in the Alzheimer's disease movement. When Wanda was diagnosed with this dreadful disorder, I immediately set out to educate myself on it. I subscribed to the national magazine and plugged into a local support group. Consequently, I've been able to minister to numerous families and individuals that have been affected by this terrible illness. In fact, I now receive letters from people seeking encouragement or insight about how to cope when a loved one is stricken with Alzheimer's.

Suddenly, I have been given another vehicle by which to share the good news of God's grace, healing, and salvation. From the ashes of tragedy, God has again given birth to something redemptive. I hope to volunteer more of my time to reach out to people who have been touched by this disease.

It's impossible to sum up fifty-seven years of marriage in a few words—or even in a whole book—but I'm blessed to have spent so many beautiful and dynamic years with Wanda Jones, my wife, lover, and co-laborer for Christ.

Because she had the courage and faith to tell me, "I love you, but I love Christ more," she helped lead me to a true relationship with Jesus Christ. And beyond that, she helped set into motion the incredible journey that would take us around the world and that would help change the face—and complexion—of American evangelism.

I thank my God upon every remembrance of you.

SEVENTEEN
Go Ye Therefore
PEOPLE, PLACES, AND ETERNAL THINGS

The problem with writing a book such as this is that you can never include all the names and places and events that make up the totality of one's life. For every memory I've recorded, I've had to leave out so many others. But in this, the final chapter, I will try to tie up some of the loose ends I see. Of course, in doing so, I'll invariably introduce more loose ends and leave out more key names, places, and events. But, hey, give an eighty-two-year-old preacher a break. I've done a lot of living!

THE PEOPLE

There are so many partners in ministry who, for one reason or another, did not make it into the previous chapters. These are people who have labored alongside me, supplied me with key moments of needed encouragement, or served as role models and quiet sources of inspiration along the way.

• Bill Watkins was a missionary to West Africa who provided me with my introduction to real missionary work. Upon my arrival in Liberia in 1957, Bill took me deep into the African bush country, where I received an education both on the desperate needs of the people hidden in the interior regions of the country and the need for the evangelist to not just kick back and broadcast the gospel from the comfort of the radio station, but to personally take it to the people where they live.

• Joe Gillespie and Walter Grist served as my crusade directors for various events both domestic and international. Their wisdom, support, and excellent organizational skills helped keep our rallies running smoothly so we could focus on winning more souls.

• Henry Davis (piano) and the late Archie Dennis (vocals) were incredible musicians who helped lead the crowds into a spirit of worship and praise at some of my international crusades.

• Jimmy Mamou is an exceptional guitarist and soloist who joined me for my meetings during the England crusade in 1984. He continues to work with the Graham Association as a member of Ralph Bell's team. And Huntley Brown is a phenomenal, up-and-coming pianist who played for me at crusade stops throughout the United States. Someday, I'm certain, you'll see Huntley's name on a list of great virtuoso piano players. His talent is boundless.

• The late Don Luttrell was a missionary pilot and the president of WIVV Christian radio, broadcast in Puerto Rico and throughout the Caribbean. Along with his wife, Ruth, Don also helped run a Bible school. During my 1977 crusade throughout the Caribbean, he graciously flew us from island to island.

• Robert Schindler, who died in 2002, was a respected surgeon and the director of ELWA's hospital. Even though the Liberian villages had their own doctors, many Africans walked great distances to see Dr. Schindler. Robert and his wife, Marion, were a lovely couple who devoted themselves to ministering to the people of Liberia.

• Bill Pannell was a young Youth for Christ leader who spoke and led music at some of my domestic crusades. Now retired, Bill was a professor of theology at Fuller Seminary in Pasadena, California, and an outspoken leader on issues of racial justice in the church.

• Mother Mae Davis was the legendary black Baptist missionary who broke barriers for race and gender in missions. Her indefatigable spirit helped label her "Africa's Woman of Faith." Her life's call was to educate and care for Liberia's abandoned children, and it was a privilege for Wanda and me to meet her during our first tour of West Africa.

• Rev. J. D. Bell for many years was the field representative for the black Alliance churches. During my years at Nyack, the a cappella group, the Gospel Crusaders, traveled to New Kensington, Pennsylvania, to sing at the large Alliance youth camp meetings there that were headed by Reverend Bell. He was a mentor and inspiration to countless people—from Bible students to established preachers.

• Torrey Johnson was president of Youth for Christ International and a popular speaker during the 1940s and 1950s. I met him in 1944 at Calvary Baptist Church in New York. Jack Wyrtzen was there doing a special service, and Torrey came with him. I went to the service to ask Jack if he'd speak at my first Soldiers for Christ youth rally. He agreed. But before I could leave, Torrey suggested we have prayer. As we prayed, he kept a hand on my shoulder. When we were finished, he said, "Howard, while I was praying, the Lord revealed to me that you will have a great ministry in Africa." I didn't know what to make of that remark at the time, but years later I looked back on that moment and thanked God for Torrey's special word of encouragement. Torrey passed away in 2002.

• E.K. Bailey, a respected brother and preacher in Dallas, Texas, invited me to speak at his popular national preaching conference back in July 2001. It was my privilege to share my story with some 1,100 African-American pastors from around the country, as I helped present an award to my dear brother Stephen Olford, who was honored at the event.

• Finally, as an associate evangelist with the BGEA and a member of the board of directors of the National Religious Broadcasters, I had the privilege over the years of meeting with five U.S. Presidents—Lyndon Johnson, Gerald Ford, Jimmy Carter, Ronald Reagan, and George H.W. Bush. And during the Queen of England's visit to Liberia in the late 1950s, Wanda and I received an official invitation from the British Embassy to attend a special reception in the Queen's honor. We were both thrilled to be a part of such a historic moment.

THE PLACES

Oh, the places the gospel will take you. A rundown of the crusades and conferences on evangelism in all the places I've visited would take more pages than I have here, but allow me to dash off some highlights: Southern Rhodesia, Swaziland, Berlin, Switzerland, Amsterdam, South Korea, the Philippines, Jamaica, the Caribbean. And the list goes on.

On the crusade trail, we faced all types of governments—from oppressive regimes and Communist hotspots to democratic nations and those still searching for a permanent system of governance. But no matter the nation or government, the people are all the same. They hunger and thirst for real hope and greater meaning in their lives. And the gospel of Jesus Christ is the answer to all they've been searching for—whether they recognize it or not. The evangelist's job is to help them recognize it.

In January 1980, I was pleased to participate in a series of crusades sponsored by churches in Jamaica and the West Indies. Ralph Bell was a featured speaker on that tour, along with associate evangelist Roy Gustafson, musical soloists Walter Arties and Steve Musto, pianists Ted Cornell and Edward Thomas, and my son David, who sang, played guitar, and generally took good care of his dad.

We conducted smaller crusades in locations such as Montego Bay and Ocho Rios, before converging on the city of Kingston for an island-wide event led by Ralph. All through the tour, it was my privilege to meet many people of all races who listened to my radio program in Jamaica and other islands in the Caribbean over TransWorld Radio, in Bonair in the Lesser Antilles. Wherever we went, thousands of people turned out and God's Spirit motivated great numbers to come forward to commit or rededicate their lives to Christ.

By God's grace, tens of thousands of souls have come to Christ through these and other crusade events. And it was my privilege to be a tiny part of what God is doing in the hearts and minds of people from around the globe.

Though the international crusades were often the more

prominent ones, my work with the Billy Graham Evangelistic Association frequently brought me to points throughout the United States and Canada. In addition to massive regional crusades, there were smaller citywide campaigns and numerous local church meetings. My domestic crusades sent me to Massachusetts, Pennsylvania, Ohio, Georgia, Wisconsin, Illinois, Washington, California, Nebraska, and on it goes.

One of my most memorable domestic meetings took place circa 1973 in a little town called Winner, South Dakota. I had been invited by a group of white evangelicals to lead a community revival. Their hope was to invite the local Native American community. Unfortunately, when the white pastors contacted the Native churches on the Sioux reservation, they said they didn't want to be a part of any event because, culturally speaking, it was "a white man's crusade." However, when the white pastor explained a black preacher from Billy Graham's team would be speaking, the Native American leaders wanted to meet me.

After ministering to the larger crusade in Winner, I journeyed out to the Sioux reservation to speak to a crowd of two hundred. It was a wonderful time, and I was invited back to an evening powwow. I was saddened, though, that there was still such a wall between the Native and white populations in that area. A few Native Americans did eventually attend the crusade meetings, but there clearly was still a long way to go. At the least, the white evangelicals were pleased that the ice had been broken. Over the years, I've often prayed that the seed planted in Winner three decades ago was able to take root and grow into a reconciled Christian community.

AND EVERYTHING ELSE

I continued to do my weekly *Hour of Freedom* radio broadcast for the Graham Association until 2001, but I officially retired from the BGEA in 1994. I will be forever grateful for the clout my connection with that organization allowed me. Being the first African American on Billy Graham's team probably will always be the first thing listed on my 'résumé.' However, the reality is that I am connected in varying degrees to a variety of other ministries as well.

One of the ministries of which I'm most proud was the Christian Family Outreach Camp, which was launched by members of my family in 1978. The camp, which was located fifty miles from Cleveland near Rock Creek, Ohio, provided weeklong camping opportunities for young people and families from around the region. Many of the camp attendees (there were about one hundred each week) were inner-city youth who would not otherwise have a chance to take part in a genuine summer camp experience. Often the kids arrived complaining that they did not want to be there, but by week's end they were crying because they did not want to leave.

The weekly agenda consisted of devotions, classes in Bible, arts and crafts, music, horseback riding, swimming, and a variety of sports. Most important, we saw many young people give their lives to Christ during one-on-one time with counselors.

The camp was truly a family affair. Andre Thornton was the President, I was the Vice President and Treasurer, Pat Kelly the Executive Director, Wanda Jones the Program Director, Lutrell Hill the Secretary, David Jones the music Director, and many others were also on the staff.

Our involvement in the camp lasted until 1991, when we turned the ministry over to another group that continues it to this day, though under another name. Still, the legacy of those thirteen years continues. Many of the kids who attended the camp have gone on to graduate from college and lead productive lives, overcoming the odds. Some of the kids have even entered into full-time ministry.

In addition to our work with Christian Family Outreach, Wanda and I traveled to several Alliance youth camps throughout Ohio and across the nation to share the Good News with young people.

Of course, my history with The Christian and Missionary Alliance Church predates anything else I've done in my fifty-nine years of public ministry. I will always be thankful for the solid spiritual foundation the C&MA provided me as a young Christian. In a day when most evangelical denominations quietly bought into society's segregationist mores, the C&MA was earnestly reaching out to blacks and other minorities. That's not to say the denomination has been perfect in its race-relations efforts. There still need to be more African-American pastors and missionaries within the ranks of the C&MA, and the group can do better at planting churches in the inner cities and other non-suburban areas. Still, I applaud the denomination for the groundbreaking moves it has made.

In 1984 the Alliance Church invited Wanda and me to tour several French-speaking African nations, including the Congo (formerly Zaire), Gabon, Mali, and Cote d'Ivoire (formerly the Ivory Coast). Those were some of our most exciting meetings, and hundreds of hearts were won for Christ.

Wanda had many opportunities to witness for her Lord. She was the first woman ever to speak to the faculty and student body of the University of Kinshasa, Zaire. In other engagements, she spoke about her conversion and her ministry to her family. Women of various racial and social backgrounds asked questions about marriage and the home. Some women, with tears in their eyes, sought counseling for their personal spiritual problems. As a result, in one country two women decided to organize a Christian women's club to meet on a regular basis.

I discovered in my public and private meetings with pastors, evangelists, and missionaries that they also needed prayer and encouragement from the Word of God for spiritual issues in their lives and ministries.

Throughout our six-week journey, many people confessed that they wore various charms, rings, and bracelets to protect themselves from the power of Satan. They had basically carried over elements of former pagan beliefs into their newfound faith in God. But after hearing our message of salvation and deliverance through the power of Christ's blood, they were able to discard those pagan idols and depend wholly on God's protection.

Radio and television enabled us to carry the gospel to thousands of people. In Abidjan, Cote d'Ivoire, our evangelistic team was on the popular *Protestant Hour,* viewed by some 3 million people throughout the nation. My messages were translated and recorded on cassette tapes and bought by people who went on to use them in home Bible studies. What's more, special concerts by the Zaire Nsangu Malamu Trio were outstanding. Thousands were blessed by the singing and guitar playing of these gifted young men.

Our final crusade was in Bamako, Mali, where some 16,000 people packed the stadium. During the event, Dr.

Dieke Koffi, president of the Alliance churches of Africa, presented Wanda and me with the colorful African chief robes, gave us African names, and stated that this honor bestowed on us was the highest given to any guest who had ever come to his country. We thanked him and gave him a big "soul brother and sister" hug, as the crowd roared with appreciation.

Later, Wanda and I were invited to visit with an American missionary couple who did Bible translation work. The wife, whom I'll call Linda, was particularly eager to chat with us. We sat together over dessert and debriefed about the various meetings. As we sipped our tea, suddenly tears began to well up in Linda's eyes. She pardoned herself as she dried her eyes with a napkin. "I'm sorry for being so emotional," she said. "My husband and I have been missionaries in this part of Africa for more than twenty years; however, in all of our time here, I never believed that American blacks would be accepted in Africa as missionaries because of the cultural factor. But tonight, as I saw the way they honored you, I was shocked with joy."

She dabbed at her eyes some more with the napkin, then continued: "Then, Howard, when you preached that powerful message and the people came forward in droves, I knew I had been wrong in my thinking about American blacks as missionaries. God showed me tonight that effectiveness on the mission field, or any other place, depends on His anointing them with His Spirit, not on the basis of their color or culture. Please forgive us for our prejudice."

We thanked Linda and her husband for their honesty and kindness, then prayed with them. We left there feeling that we had made a new friend—and helped shatter a sad misconception that was once embraced by many white members of the C&MA and other denominations as well.

I am still a member of the Alliance Church in Oberlin. Our pastor, Reverend Charles Mayle is ninety-four years old, retired, but still active in the church. On any given Sunday you might find me preaching the sermon, teaching Sunday school, or leading an impromptu board meeting. The work of the church is still in my blood, and the little Alliance congregation is home.

I have received various honors over the years. One of the most memorable is the Hall of Fame award bestowed upon me by the National Religious Broadcasters in 1996. I was the first African American to receive this award. Then there's the honorary doctorate that I received from Huntington College in Huntington, Indiana (my son's undergraduate alma mater). Things like these always help to boost one's spirits (and his ego, if he's not careful), but I try to keep these types of tributes in perspective.

Perhaps one of the greatest honors of my ministry career was the Howard O. Jones Chair of Evangelism established by Crown College in St. Paul, Minnesota, during the late 1980s. I had been a regular speaker at Crown's chapel services in the 1970s before becoming an adjunct faculty member and teaching occasional classes on evangelism, preaching, and racial reconciliation between semesters. So it meant a lot for that school to bestow that honor upon me.

Each year, the Chair grants a generous scholarship to a student who feels led to go into missions or evangelism. I'm proud to be involved in the training and edification of our future leaders on the mission and evangelism circuit, and that's probably why this honor stands out a little bit above the others.

When you're a cut-and-dry evangelist, it's easy to get lost in the crowd of dynamic preachers. Many of the top preachers today are known for homiletical flair or colorful teaching. My preaching has always been defined, first and foremost, by the simple truth of the gospel.

As an evangelical preacher, I loved what I did. I loved to share the Word of God, and I did it with as much gusto and passion and emotion as I could muster. But never did I enter that colorful realm of whooping or hooping (depending on where you're from). I was from Ohio, after all. That's not to say I couldn't get into the spirit of it; it just isn't who I am. I'm a more understated preacher who lets the Word of God do the serious shouting. In my ministry, I was always just the conduit, the channel by which God could either blare or whisper His words.

In 1965 I was named the second president of the National Black Evangelical Association (NBEA; founded in 1963); I served that organization faithfully until two years later when the Black Power movement emerged as a dominant voice in the black community. I had always been a strong supporter of civil rights in the vein of Dr. King; however, the Black Power movement demanded a more aggressive and nationalistic stand on issues of racial justice—and a black man who worked for Billy Graham clearly seemed out of step with the direction the movement was going. Not everyone in the NBEA looked down upon my affiliation with Graham. But the small number of folks who *did* made a lot of noise, and I decided to leave that post in 1967.

In those days, I lost a lot of black friends who thought I should leave Billy's organization. But I knew the right thing was to stay. My black brothers and sisters who accuse Billy of not being vocal enough against racism and other social issues have not seen what goes on behind the scenes at the BGEA. They do not know Billy's heart.

I may be accused of being "old school" or a Graham loyalist, but I believe my record on issues of racial justice should speak for itself. I've never forgotten that I'm a black man working in a predominantly white world. In fact, I've been confronted with that fact one way or another each day of my life. The question is, *What am I going to do with that reality?* Some folks choose bitterness and division; I believe in grace and reconciliation. I believe that is how Christ would have us respond.

Rather than curse someone's flickering light, I think we should go out of our way to encourage positive things being done. For instance, one of my most important and heartrending trips with the BGEA was our 1973 mission to drought-stricken nations of North Africa, where more than thirteen million people were starving to death. The Graham organization raised more than $100,000 (a pretty good sum back in 1973) to help aid famine-relief efforts in Mali, Chad, Upper Volta, Senegal, Niger, and Mauritania. Those are the kinds of constructive efforts sadly overlooked when one sees the world with a myopic vision that is eager to criticize but slow to praise.

WHAT ARE WE WAITING FOR?

But don't get me wrong. I think there's a place for an honest and intelligent critique of the American evangelical church's efforts in areas of diversity and social justice. The truth is, we haven't done enough to build solid bridges between the races. We have not done enough to minister to the poor and needy in our own country. If evangelical churches had been as devoted to reaching the American inner cities fifty years ago as they were to reaching Africa and other international spots, the United States would probably look a lot different.

I don't think a church has any justification for being in existence if it's working overseas among a people of color yet cannot marshal the love to work among their counterparts here in the States. It doesn't make sense.

You may recall that during Billy's New York crusade in 1957, many of the evangelical leaders told him, "Don't go to Harlem. Those savages will kill you." These were white *pastors* talking. Yet they were the same ones sending missionaries to Third World nations to spread the gospel. Does that make any sense? No wonder we have growing numbers of black groups who are rejecting Christianity and rejecting the church.

But I digress. Let me say it again: Our only hope is Jesus Christ. We are so good at introducing politics and ideologies and culture and race into our presentations of the Christian faith. But when you strip away all that man-made baggage, all that is left is the gospel, the simple message of the Cross, which says: "Come to me, all you who are weary and burdened, and I will give you rest. Take my yoke upon you and learn from me, for I am gentle and humble in heart, and you will find rest for your souls. For my yoke is easy and my burden is light" (Matt. 11:28–30).

And: "Go and make disciples of all nations . . ." (Matt. 28:19).

And: "There is neither Jew nor Greek, slave nor free, male nor female, for you are all one in Christ Jesus" (Gal. 3:28).

And: "For God so loved the world, that he gave his only begotten Son, that whosoever believeth in him should not perish, but have everlasting life" (John 3:16, KJV).

This, in essence, is what my ministry has always been about. Little did I realize when I gave my life to Jesus Christ sixty-two years ago that He would use me in the ways that He has. God has given me the privilege to serve as His ambassador to audiences in the United States and abroad. He blessed me with fifty-seven years of marriage to a one-of-a-kind woman and five wonderful children who have chosen to walk with Christ. I didn't earn or deserve any of these things, yet God gave them to me anyway. I am a humbled beneficiary of this boundless love and grace.

For God so loved the world that He gave . . .

It is this profound truth that gets me up in the morning and keeps me going. I fully realize my weaknesses, my failures, my lack of trust. But God's grace is more than sufficient. His Word is my strong tower. Therefore, I am determined to let Him use my entire life for His glory until Jesus comes.

Here I am, Lord . . . Here I am.

WANDA KATHLEEN JONES

Wanda Kathleen Jones, 78, a lifelong resident of Oberlin, died Thursday, November 8, at Oberlin Medical Center following a long illness.

On the evening of Sunday, November 11th, we had the wake. The floral display enhanced the beauty of the room. People came from all over town and across the country to attend Wanda's service. At the conclusion of the wake, my son, David, called the immediate members of the family together for one last look at the body that once held our dear wife and mother. We prayed, thanking God for the gift of her life, employing Him to keep her legacy alive in our hearts and various ministries.

The graveside service was on November 12th at 9:00 A.M. at Westwood Cemetery in Oberlin, Ohio.

Later in the morning at 11:00 A.M. Wanda's memorial service was held at the First Church of Oberlin. Ralph Bell offered the invocation and shared some personal remarks. Cheryl and David offered poignant reflections of their mother. The obituary was read by our granddaughter, April Kelly. Reverend Mayle delivered the eulogy, and Cheryl's husband, Norman Sanders closed in prayer.

One of the hymns we sang that morning was *All the Way My Savior Leads Me,* which was a song Wanda and I used to sing in a duet. It was one of the themes of our life together.

And now in view of Wanda's homegoing with the Lord, please pray for me and the rest of the family that we'll fulfill the ministry He's called us to, and help hasten the return of our Lord.

Steps to Peace With God

1. RECOGNIZE GOD'S PLAN—PEACE AND LIFE

   The message in this book stresses that God loves you
   and wants you to experience His peace and life.

   The BIBLE says ... For God loved the
   world so much that He gave His only Son,
   so that everyone who believes in Him may
   not die but have eternal life. John 3:16

2. REALIZE OUR PROBLEM—SEPARATION

   People choose to disobey God and go their
   own way. This results in separation from God.

   The BIBLE says ... Everyone has
   sinned and is far away from God's saving
   presence. Romans 3:23

3. RESPOND TO GOD'S REMEDY—CROSS OF CHRIST

   God sent His Son to bridge the gap. Christ
   did this by paying the penalty of our sins when
   He died on the cross and rose from the grave.

   The BIBLE says ... But God has shown
   us how much He loves us—it was while we
   were still sinners that Christ died for us!
   Romans 5:8

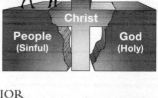

4. RECEIVE GOD'S SON—LORD AND SAVIOR

   You cross the bridge into God's family when
   you ask Christ to come into your life.

   The BIBLE says ... Some, however, did
   receive Him and believed in Him; so He
   gave them the right to become God's
   children. John 1:12

THE INVITATION IS TO:

REPENT (turn from your sins) and by faith RECEIVE Jesus Christ into your
heart and life and follow Him in obedience as your Lord and Savior.

PRAYER OF COMMITMENT

"Lord Jesus, I know I am a sinner. I believe You died for my sins. Right now, I turn
from my sins and open the door of my heart and life. I receive You as my personal
Lord and Savior. Thank You for saving me now. Amen."

If you are committing your life to Christ, please let us know!
Billy Graham Evangelistic Association
1 Billy Graham Parkway, Charlotte, NC 28201-0001
1-877-2GRAHAM (1-877-247-2426)
www.billygraham.org